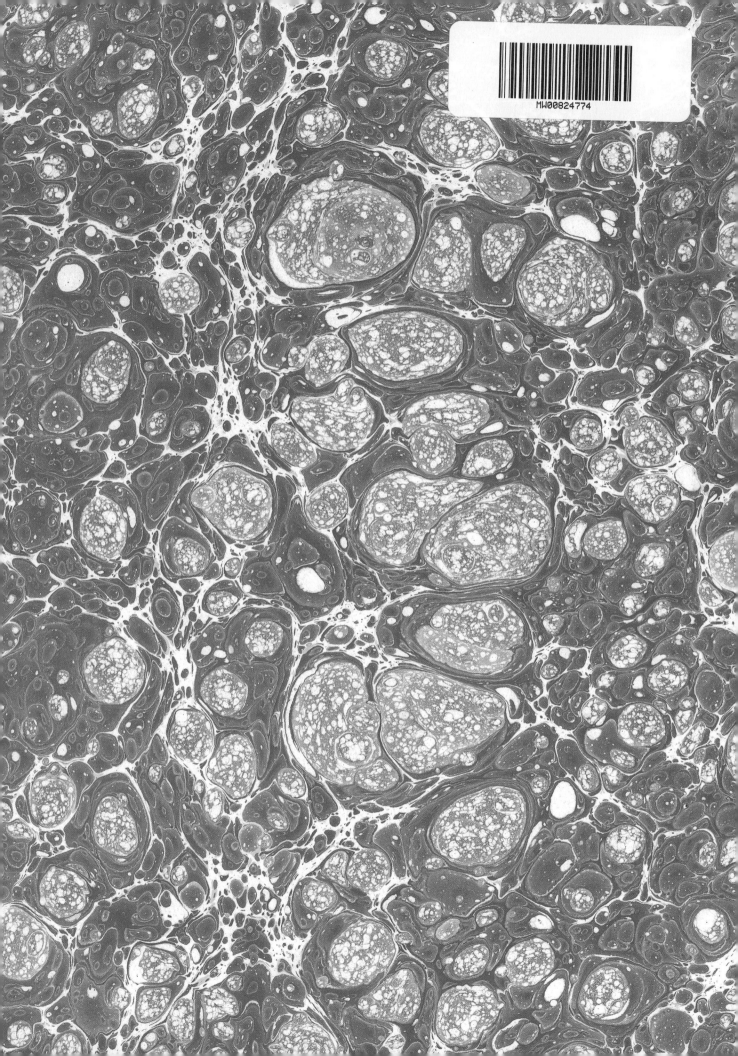

THE LUFTWAFFE
FROM TRAINING SCHOOL TO THE FRONT

THE LUFTWAFFE

FROM TRAINING SCHOOL TO THE FRONT

An Illustrated Study 1933-1945
Michael Meyer & Paul Stipdonk

Schiffer Military/Aviation History
Atglen, PA

Dustjacket artwork by Steve Ferguson, Colorado Springs, CO.

SORTIE TO SOUTH HAMPTON

In the epic Battle of Britain, Germany's Luftwaffe executed an aerial onslaught never before seen in warfare. As of October, 1940, the *Jagdflieger* proved they were the finest fighter force in the world and likely would have vanquished the depleted RAF fighter command had their aircraft been equal to the final logistical assault on England. Depicted here is a mid-November fighter escort for Bf 110 fighter-bombers bound for shipping at South Hampton, a target that was at the very extreme limit of the superlative Bf 109. In the foreground is the *stabkette* of JG 2 *Richthofen* accompanied by two elements of I. *Gruppe* being led by the *Geschwaderkommodore Major* Helmut Wick. In just four months of combat, Wick had advanced from *staffelkapitän* to the command of his *Gruppe*, certainly due to his leadership skills, but likewise because of the staggering losses of command grade pilots. Fiercely competitive and driven by the glory of commendations, Wick would be the youngest fighter pilot to reach the rank of *major* and later *kommodore*, while likewise joining fellow aces Werner Mölders and Adolph Galland as the only *Jagdfliegern* to win the Oak Leaves to the Knight's Cross. As of late November, he had led all combatants with a victory count of fifty only to be killed in a duel with Spitfires off the Isle of Wight on November 28th. His loss pointedly underscored the woeful list of casualties from which the Luftwaffe would never fully recover.

This book was originally published under the title,
*Von der Fliegerschule zum Einsatzverband:
Ein Bildband der deutschen Luftwaffe, 1933-1945*
by Flugzeug Publikations GmbH.

Copyright © 1996 by Schiffer Publishing Ltd.
Library of Congress Catalog Number: 95-72485

Printed in China.
ISBN: 0-88740-924-5

We are interested in hearing from authors with book ideas on related topics.

Published by Schiffer Publishing Ltd.
77 Lower Valley Road
Atglen, PA 19310
Please write for a free catalog.
This book may be purchased from the publisher.
Please include $2.95 postage.
Try your bookstore first.

CONTENTS

Plates

FOREWORD

One can't even depend on its own prejudice anymore!," one of our old pilots remarked when he came to know the two young authors better after he met them at our FLIEGERTREFF (Pilot's Meet) in Hamburg – the German Michael Meyer and the Dutchman Paul G. Stipdonk. Most everybody considered them as "photo collectors" or similar types, scrounging for whole inheritances to resell them and make a fast buck. But the visitors of the "Kleinen Gartenzaun Hamburg," pilots technicians, etc., of various Luftwaffe units and the industry, in short all participants of the then aviation, quickly learned that these young lads were often more knowledgeable about developments, trials, aircraft, weapons, implements, markings, or units and operations, than themselves; and that their selective questions proved their profound knowledge and interest. Agreeably, almost everyone made their photos, documents and other papers available, at least for reproduction or photostats, to help them complete a comprehensive documentation.

This task, into which both invested not only much off-time and immense efforts but also considerable funds, is by far not complete. It is to be hoped that this publishing will induce as many people as possible to furnish their documents etc. – even if seemingly unimportant – to help establish a most complete picture of German aviation of the World War II years, for those after us and ourselves, too.

Hellmut Detjens
former pilot JG 4 and JG 7

INTRODUCTION

After nearly ten years of intensive research work on the history of the German Luftwaffe, the authors finally decided to present a selection of our collected pictures to other aviation enthusiasts.

The idea of producing such a book stemmed from former members of the Luftwaffe and our modelling friends. To publish a book on the Luftwaffe today involves (perhaps) certain risks. With some people, it can possibly create the impression of having an obsession with the connotations surrounding the Third Reich or worse. Others might say that a pictorial study on aircraft showing swastikas on their tails is still a "hot" and controversial topic, even though more than fifty years have passed since the last aircraft with such markings were in operational use. The incorrigible, finally, might relish the symbols, the convinced pacifist might shake his head. Former members of the Luftwaffe, modelers, aviation enthusiasts and historians, however will surely evaluate this book differently. The interest for these men, their aircraft and the Luftwaffe's history from 1933-1945 is solely founded on a historic basis. We who both belong to the post-war generation, are neither weapons fanatics nor glorifiers of war. Our study presented here is enough proof of this. With a love for details and a fascination for a bygone technology, the photos shown here have been carefully selected. Not only the highly decorated "aces" are featured, but also the indispensable ground crew who provided us with many of the photos printed in the study. The shots included show the ground crew at work or proudly presenting "their" planes.

The machines flown by pilots without the Knight's Cross are, however, the central theme of the book. Somewhere and somehow every pilot had learned to fly, regardless of how highly decorated he was later. Thus the pilot training schools will also find their section in this book. Some of them will be mentioned for the very first time, others are well-knowr Additionally, we publish a list of Geschwader codes which have remained a mystery until now; the reader is also kindly asked for assistance.

The stylish fighters are presented in their various roles, including their different liveries and victory rudder markings – not only those of the "aces" but also of the innumerable pilots who lost their lives in the hell of the Western and Eastern sky. Another section focuses on the dive bombers and close support units, reconnaissance aircraft, and transport units which flew their self-sacrificing missions and were shot down over Stalingrad, Crete and in the Demjansk battle – among them awful massacres took place in the Mediterranean theater. Often, recovery and air-rescue missions conducted by naval aircrews meant the only chance at survival.

Former Luftwaffe members, whether flying personnel or technicians, might perhaps recognize comrades or "their" machine.

Another interesting chapter focuses on aircraft bought or captured abroad. Among them are highlights for both the aviation historian and the modeler. Especially the latter, as they will surely find new subjects for reproduction in miniature. To all plastic modelers we are proud to offer many new details which have been un-

Photography strictly forbidden!
Fortunately for us, many aviation enthusiasts disregarded the notice shown above strictly forbidding photography and pressed the

known until now. The historian, though, might find some valuable clues to all the questions unsolved.

With the photos, we put a strong emphasis on historically correct and fundamental captions. To avoid any mistakes, we dispensed with the detailed designation of possible sub-variants of a particular aircraft. For example, take the exhausting variety of the Messerschmitt Bf 109G: Ranging from G-0 to G-14, even the serial number does not allow the specialist to differentiate a F-5 from a G-6 or a G-6/R-6 AS beyond any doubts. Thus we confine ourselves to the designation Bf 109G. Details as such and further information on the aircraft's color scheme are to be found in the relevant reference literature listed elsewhere in this publication.

The attentive reader will notice the partly vague captioning of several pictures. This is primarily due to the fact that after forty years the memories of ex-Luftwaffe members has begun to fade. Who can blame them? Additionally, quite a few photos were handed in without any further guideline or caption so that retriev-

ing the necessary background material often required criminalistic skills. To close this gap we have to rely on the assistance and support of our readers.

If memories come floating back when discovering a certain aircraft in this book please do not hesitate to contact us. Perhaps you recognize a code, a machine, an aircraft's side rudder, the pilot's name etc. Of course we are also liable to mistakes, so do not hesitate to correct us. Write to us courtesy of the publisher, if you would like to address a question to us.

When giving units, always indicate the group by Roman and the squadron in Arabic characters. Future documentation and research work depends very much on new material. We therefore would like to ask our readers to lend us their photo albums or negatives. Perhaps some gaps could then be closed.

We hope you will enjoy reading this book and gratefully acknowledge any future help.

Paul G. Stipdonk
Borgholzhausen, January 1992

German Air Force Unit Codes, 1933-1945

The following list attempts to present all codes known so far in alphabetical order. This compilation, however, must still be regarded as incomplete.

A1+	KG 53
A2+	I./ZG 52 (From July 6, 1940 onwards): II./ZG 2, Flugbereitschaft Kd. Gen. d. dt. L. in Finnland
A3+	KG 200, Versuchskdo. 200, Versuchskdo. 36
A4+	
A5+	I./St.G.1, SG 1
A6+	Aufkl.Gr.120
A8+	
B1+	Transportstaffel I./Fliegerkorps (occasionally also called Transport Squadron "Don")
B3+	KG 54
B4+	Nachtjagdstaffel Finland
B7+	
C1+	E-Stelle Peenemünde (Me 163)
C2+	Aufkl.Gr.41
C3+	Transportstaffel II. Fliegerkorps
C5+	
C6+	KGrzbV. 600, Tr.Fl.St.4
C8+	I.+II. KGrzbV. 323, TG 5 (5 Transport Wing)
C9+	NJG 5
D1+	SAGr.126, LD.Kdo.65
D3+	Nachtschlachtgruppe 2
D5+	NJG 3, frequently also with the code
L1+	
D7+	Wekusta 5 (from April 1943 onwards in connection with the code letter "N", previously 1B+ with the squadron letter "H")
D9+	Nachtjagdstaffel Norwegen, temporarily I./NJG 7
E1-E7+	E-Stelle Rechlin (for Me 163 and Ar 234)
E8+	I./FKG 50
F1+	KG 76, I./St.G.76; using the letter C,M,N,P of the II. Gruppe as those of the I. Gruppe had already been allocated to the I./KG 76 and, from July 6, 1940 onwards, to the III./St.G.77)
F2+	Erg.(F) Gr.
F3+	Aufkl.Gr.12
F5+	NAG 5
F6+	Aufkl.Gr.122
F7+	I./LLG 2, SAGr. 130; frequently also with the code 6I+)
F8+	KG 40, Transportstaffel "Condor"
G1+	KG 55
G2+	Aufkl.Gr.124
G3+	3./NJG 101
G5+	Transportstaffel V. Fliegerkorps
G6+	KGrzbV. 2; 101, 102, 103, 104 & 105, TG 4, 1st Lufttransport Gruppe See 1 (Maritime)
G8+	Transportstaffel IV. Fliegerkorps
G9+	NJG 1, ZG 1 (initial formation), NJG 4; only for a short period of time)
H1+	Aufkl.Gr.12
H4+	LLG 1
H7+	St.G.3, SG 3
H8+	Aufkl.Gr.33
H9+	Lufttransportstaffel See 7 (Maritime)

J2+	NAG 3
J4+	Lufttransportstaffel 5 and 290
J6+	KGrzbV. 500
J9+	St.G.5, SG 5, previously I.(T)/ St.G.186, carrier-based, from July 6, 1940 onward III./St.G.1)
K1+	Kurierstaffel of Ob.d.L.
K6+	Küfl.Gr.406, KG 6
K7+	Aufkl.Gr.Nacht
K9+	Aufkl.Gr.B.d.L. (also T5+)
L1+	I./NJG 3, I. and IV.(Z)/LG 1, and I./ St.G.5 (also IV.(St.)/LG 1) (also I./ St.G.5, former IV.(St.)/LG 1
L2+	LG 2
L5+	KGrzbV.5,7./Erg.Transport-G(7./Erg. Transportgeschwader)
L7+	Seen with +AB-AF on a Fi 156, Bf 108 and Bf 110
M2+	Küfl.Gr.106
M3+	Seen on a Ju 52/3m (unit?)
M7+	Küfl.Gr.806
M8+	ZG 76 (first activation)
N1+	Grossraumtransportstaffel ab January 30, 1945
N3+	I./KGrzbV.172 (also 4V+)
N6+	Verband Major Babekuhl
N7+	Sseen on a Do 18 (Unit?)
N9+	Flugbereitschaft Norwegen
P1+	KGr.60
P2+	Aufkl.Gr.21
P4+	Führungskette X.Fliegerkorps, Transportstaffel Fliegerführer Nord (Ost)
P5+	Sonderstaffel Trans-Ozean, KGr.zbV.108, Kdo.d.Transportfl. Chef See-Norwegen
Q5+	Westa 27 to)ctober 1943. Thereafter 5M+ with Westa 26/Lfl.2 in Southern Greece.

R4+	NJG 2 to the summer of 1944. Thereafter 4R+.
S1+	St.G.3 (also S7+)
S2+	St.G.77, SG 77
S3+	KGrzbV.5, Transportgruppe 30
S4+	KüflGr. 506
S7+	St.G.3, SG 3
S9+	Zunächst Erp.Gr.210, (at first Erp.Gr.210 until April 1941, then SKG 210 and from 1942 on ZG 1 gether with 2N+)
T1+	Aufkl.Gr. 10
T3+	1./Bordfliegerstaffel 196
T5+	Aufkl.St.Ob.d.L, 3.(Einsatz) Ob.d. Aufkl.Gr.100, (with last letter U m teorological Squadron Commande in-Chief Luftwaffe)
T6+	St.G.2, SG 2 (with Z as last letter Dive Bomber Replacement Trainir Squadron of VIII. Fliegerkorps).
T9+	Versuchsverband (Transport) d.OK II./Versuchsverband Commander-i Chief Luftwaffe = Circus Rosariou several special commandos.
U2+	Nachtrotte of NAG 5
U4+	KG 2
U8+	I./ZG 26 (Erstaufstellung) (Initial A tivation
U9+	NSG 3

V1+	Transportstaffel VIII. Fliegerkorps
V3+	Seen on a Ju 88
V4+	KG 1
V7+	Aufkl.Gr.32 (during the war they patially used an own code: the squadron number was immediately right of the Balkenkreuz, followed by the let ter indicating the aircraft within the unit, e.g. V7+2G was aircraft "G" within the unit).
W1-W3+	Me 321 unit
W5+	Me 321 unit
W7+	Me 321 unit, NJG 100
W8-W9+	Me 321 unit
X4+	Lufttransportstaffel (See) 222, later also SAGr. 129
X8+	Flugbereitschaft RLM Staaken
Z4+	Transportstaffel III. Fliegerkorp
Z5+	Seen on Do 17 (unit unknown)
Z6+	KG 66
1B+	13.(Z)/JG 5 (only in connection with "X" as the final code letter), Westa Luftflotte 5 (only in connection with "H" as the final letter)
1G+	KG 27
1H+	KG 26
1K+	NSGr.4
1L+	Seen on a Bf 110, Ju 88 and He 219
1R+	Kurierstaffel in Finland (perhaps Kurierstaffel AOK Lapland?)
1T+	KG 28, KGr.126
1Z+	KGrzbV.1, TG 1 Savoia Staffel, III./KGrzbV.1
2B+	2.Fligerschuledivision
2F+	KG 54 (Until March 1940), 5./KG 28
2H+	Versuchsstaffel 210
2J+	ZG 1 (after reforming)
2N+	ZG 76 (after reforming. Originally II./ZG 1, from July 1940 onwards III./ZG 76)
2P+	X. Fliegerdivision
2S+	I/ZG 2 (after reforming)

2Z+	NJG 6 (from August 1943 onwards)
3C+	NJG 4, NJG 6 (July 1, 1943)
3E+	KG 6
3J+	NJG 3 (also labelled D5+)
3K+	Minensuchgruppe of the Luftwaffe
3M+	ZG 2 (initial formation)
3U+	ZG 26 (initial formation. Also used as ferry aircraft by JG 6 from August 1944 onwards)
3W+	NSG 11
3X+	I./KG 1 (originally until September 18, 1939) I./KG 152
3Z+	KG 77 (perhaps temporarily also called KG 153)
4A+	IV/ZG 26 (after the dissolution of ZG 26): in Norway, early August 1944
4B+	Westa 3
4D+	KG 30, I./KG 25
4E+	Aufkl.Gr.13 (later NAG 15)
4F+	KGr.z.b.V.400
4M+	Erg.z.Gr. (later I./SG 152)
4N+	Aufkl.Gr.22
4Q+	7./Fliegerdivision
4R+	7./NJG 2
4T+	Westa 51
4U+	Aufkl.Gr.123

4V+	KGr.z.b.V.9&KGr.z.b.V.106,I. KGr.z.b.V.172, KGr.z.b.V. Naples, TG 3, TG 4 (in April 1945)		9G+	Ju 52 Formations

4V+ KGr.z.b.V.9&KGr.z.b.V.106,I. KGr.z.b.V.172, KGr.z.b.V. Naples, TG 3, TG 4 (in April 1945)

5B+ Nachtschlachtgruppe (i.e. the renamed II./ LLG 1 as from September 1944)
5D+ Aufkl.Gr.31
5F+ Aufkl.Gr.14 (ater also called NAG 14)
5J+ KG 1
5K+ KG 3
5M+ Westa 26 Lfl.2

5T+ KSG 1 (from February 1, 1943 onwards), KG 101
5W+ Seetransportgruppe
5Z+ Wekusta 26

6A+ NAG 12
6G+ St.G.51, the original designation. III./ St.G.51 was still kept after reforming to II./St.G. 1 on July 6, 1940
6H+ Flieger Erg.Gr. (See) Kamp
6I+ Kü.Fl.Fr.706, KGr.z.b.V.108, TG 20, SAGr.130
6K+ Aufkl.Gr.23
6M+ Küstenstaffel Crimea, Aufkl.Gr.11, plus several machines of NAG 8 at the end of the war
6N+ KG 100 (machines with the squadron letter "R" were assigned to the Erprobungs- and Lehrkommando 17)

9G+ Ju 52 Formations
9K+ KG 51
9N+ Seen on Fi 156 (Unit unknown)
9P+ KGrzbV. 9, 40, 50, 60, Frankfurt & Wittstock
9V+ FAG 5
9W+ NJG 101

6Q+ Ergänzugstaffel St.G.2
6R+ SAGr. 127
6U+ ZG 1 (after reforming)
6W+ SAGr. 128, Bordfliegergruppe 128
6Z+ Transportgruppe Herzog 1945

7A+ Aufkl. Gr. 121
7J+ NJG 102
7R+ SAGr.125
7T+ KüFl.Gr.606, KGr.606
7U+ KGr.z.b.V.108
7V+ KGr.z.b.V.700

8A+ Lufttransportgruppe (See) 1
8I+ 3./(H) Pz., NAG 16
8L+ KüFlGr.906
8Q+ Transportgruppe 10, seen also on SM 82 (unit unknown)
8T+ KGr.z.b.V.800, later renamed TG 2
8U+ Stab "Transportfliegerführer 2"
8V+ NJG 200

Key to Luftwaffe designations

A unit designation, when read from the left, begins with an Arabic character for the Staffel or a Roman numeral for the Gruppe. This is followed by the name of the parent unit in abbreviated form. Providing the number of squadrons within the Geschwader is previously known, the Staffel number will indicate the Gruppe to which the it belonged.

The general rule was:
Arabic characters indicate the Staffel
Roman numerals indicate the Gruppe

For example:

7./JG 2	7 Staffel of Jagdgeschwader 2
III./LG 1	3 Gruppe of Lehrgeschwader 1
Stab I./JG 27	Staff of 1 Gruppe of JG 27
3./KüFl.Gr.506	3 Staffel of Küstenfliegergruppe 506
II./St.G.1	2 Gruppe of Stukageschwader 1
3./KGr.z.b.V.101	3 Staffel of Kampfgruppe zur besonderen Verwendung 101
I./(F)120	1 Staffel of Fernaufklärergruppe 120

Abbreviations

Ar.	Arado-Flugzeugwerke
Adju.	Adjutant
Aufkl.Gr.	Aufklärergruppe/Reconnaissance Group
BO.	Beobachter/Observer
BF.	Bordfunker/Radio Operator
BM.	Bordmechaniker/Flight Engineer
BS.	Bordschütze/Gunner
BV.	Blohm & Voss (Aircraft and ship company in Hamburg)
DB.	Daimler Benz
DFS.	Deutsche Forschungsgesellschaft-für Segelflug/German Research Institute for Gliding Flight
Do.	Dornier-Flugzeugwerke
E.Gr.	Erprobungsgruppe/Proving- or Test Group
Erg.St.	Ergänzungsstaffel/Replacement Squadron
Erg.Gr.	Ergänzungsgruppe/Replacement Group
Eis.	Eisenbahnbekämpfungsstaffel/Antitrain Attack Squadron
F.	Fernaufklärer/Long-range reconnaissance
FAGr.	Fernaufklärer/Long-range reconnaissance Group
FEA.	Fliegerersatzabteilung/WWI Pilot replacement unit which provided new pilots with operational training
FFS.	Flugzeugführerschule/Pilot training school
Fl.K	FLiegerkorps/Air Corps
Fl.Ü.G.	Fliegerüberführungsgeschwader/Luftwaffe Ferry Wing
FF.	Flugzeugführer/Pilot
Fw.	Feldwebel/Equivalent to the rank of Sergeant (R.A.F.) or Airman 1st Class (U.S.A.A.F.)
FuG.	Funkgerät/Radio telephone (R/T)
Gefr.	Gefreiter/Leading Aircraftsman (R.A.F.) or Airman 3rd Class (U.S.A.A.F.)
Gen.	General/General

Gen.Feldm.	Generalfeldmarschall/Equivalent of Air Marshal of the R.A.F. or General of the Air Force (U.S.A.A.F.)
Gen.Lt. Vice	Generalleutnant/Equivalent of Air Marshal (R.A.F.) or Major General (U.S.A.A.F.)
Gen.Maj.	Generalmajor/Equivalent to Air Commodore (R.A.F.) or Brigadier General (U.S.A.A.F.)
Gen.Oberst	Generaloberst/Equivalent to Air Chief Marshal (R.A.F.) or General (U.S.A.A.F.)
Gr.	Gruppe/Group
Go.	Gothaer Waggonfabrik
H.	Heeresaufklärer, Nahaufklärer/Army Reconnaissance, short-range reconnaissance
Ha.	Hamburger Flugzeugbau (Blohm & Voss)
He.	Heinkel-Flugzeugwerke
Hptm.	Hauptmann/Flight Lieutenant (R.A.F.) or Captain (U.S.A.A.F.)
Hs.	Henschel-Flugzeugwerke
Jabo.	Jagdbomber/Fighter Bomber
JG.	Jagdgeschwader/Fighter-Bomber Wing
Ju.	Junkers-Flugzeugwerke
Jumo.	Junkers-Motorenwerke
Kdo.	Kommando/Detachment
Kdore.	Kommodore/Commodore
Kdr.	Kommandeur/Commander
KflGr.	Küstenfliegergruppe/Naval Aviation Wing
KG.	Kampfgeschwader/Bomber Wing
LD.	Luftdienst/WWII Luftwaffe courier service
Lfl.	Luftflotte/Air fleet
LG.	Lehrgeschwader/Trainings or Instructional Wing
LKS.	Luftkriegsschule/"Air Combat School" i.e. WWII term for Luftwaffe officer school
LLG.	Luftlandegeschwader/Air-borne Wing
Ln.Sch.	Luftnachrichtenschule/Air Force Communication School
Lt.	Leutnant/Lieutenant

Maj.	Major/Major	RLM.	Reichsluftfahrtministerium/State Ministry of Aviation
Me./Bf.	Messerschmitt-Flugzeugwerke	SAGr.	Seeaufklärergruppe/Maritime Re connaissance Group
NAG.	Nahaufklärergruppe/Short-range re connaissance Group	Sd.Kdo.	Sonderkommando/Special Command
NJG.	Nachtjagdgeschwader/Night Fighter Wing	SG.	Schlachtgeschwader/Assault Wing
NSG.	Nachtschlachtgeschwader/Night Harassment Wing	SKG. High	Schnelles Kampfgeschwader/lit.: Speed Battle Wing
NSGr.	Nachtschlachtgruppe/Night Harass-ment Group	St.Kptn. mander	Staffelkapitän/Squadron Com-
		TG. Wing	Transportgeschwader/Transport
Ob.d.L.	Oberbefehlshaber der Luftwaffe/ Commander in Chief of the Luftwaffe	TGr.	Transportgruppe/Transport Group
		TO.T	echnischer Offizier/Technical Of ficer
Oblt.	Oberleutnant/Flying Officer		
Ofw.	Oberfeldwebel/Flight Sergeant (R.A.F.) Flight Lieutenant (U.S.A.A.F.)	Uffz.	Unteroffizier/Corporal
OKL.	Oberkommando Luftwaffe/Luftwaffe High Command	WL.	Wehrmacht Luftwaffe
		Westa	Wetterstaffel
Oberstlt.	Oberstleutnant/Lieutenant-Colonel	z.b.V.	zur besonderen Verwendung/for special operations
Pz.	Panzerabwehrstaffel/Anti-Tank Squadron	ZG.	Zerstörergeschwader/Destroyer Wing or Heavy Fighter Wing

Sources

a.) German publications

Aders, Gebhard, *Die Geschichte der deutschen Nachtjagd*, Motorbuch-Stuttgart 1977

–, *Stukas, Jagdbomber, Schlachflieger*, Held Werner, Motorbuch-Stuttgart 1980

Balke, Ulf *KG 100 "Wiking," Kriegstagebücher*, Motorbuch-Stuttgart 1981

Boehme, Manfred, *Jagdgeschwader 7, Chronik eines Me 262, Geschwaders 1944-1945*, Motorbuch-Stuttgart 1983

Brütting, Georg, *Das waren die deutschen Stuka-Asse 1939-1945*, Motorbuch-Stuttgart 1977

–, *Das waren die deutschen Kampfflieger-Asse 1939-1945*, Motorbuch-Stuttgart 1975

Cartier, Raymond, *Der zweite Weltkrieg* Band I+II, R. Piper Verlag-München

Dierich, Wolfgang, *KG 51 "Edelweiss"* Chronik, Motorbuch-Stuttgart 1974, 3. Auflage

–, *KG 55 "Greif"* Chronik, Motorbuch-Stuttgart 1975

–, *Die Verbände der Luftwaffe, Dokumentation*, Motorbuch-Stuttgart 1976

Forell, Fritz von *Mölders und seine Männer*, Biografie, Steirische-Graz 1941

Girbig, Werner, *JG 5 "Eismeerjäger," Chronik*, Motorbuch-Stuttgart 1976, 2. Aufl.

–, *JG 27, Dokumentation*, Ring, Hans, Motorbuch-Stuttgart 1979, 6. Aufl.

Held, Werner, *Die deutsche Tagjagd, Bildchronik*, Motorbuch-Stuttgart 1978, 2. Aufl.

–, *Der Jagdflieger Walter Nowotny*, Motorbuch-Stuttgart 1984

–, *Die deutsche Nachtjagd*, Bildchronik Nauroth, Holger, Motorbuch-Stuttgart

Hiller, Dr. Alfred, Heinkel He 162 "Volksjäger" Verlag Dr. Alfred Hiller-Wien 1984

Kens, Karlheinz, Die deutschen Flugzeuge von 1933-1945 Nowarra, Heinz J.J.F. Lehmanns-Verlag-München 1977, 5. Aufl.

Kössler, Karl *Transporter & wer kennt sie schon!* Alba Buchverlag-Düsseldorf 1976

Kühl, Heinz, *Kampfgeschwader "Legion Condor" 53*, Chronik, Motorbuch-Stuttgart 1983

Kurowski, Franz, *Luftbrücke Stalingrad*, Kurt Vowinckel-Verlag-Berg am See

Lange, Bruno, *Das Buch der deutschen Luftfahrttechnik*, Hoffmann-Verlag-Mainz 1970

Morzik, Fritz, Die deutschen Transportflieger im Zweiten Weltkrieg, Hümmelchen, Gerhard Bernard & Graefe-Frankfurt 1966

Nowarra, Heinz J., *Die Ju 88...und ihre Folgemuster*, Motorbuch-Stuttgart 1978

Obermaier, Ernst, *Die Ritterkreuzträger der Luftwaffe-Stuka & Schlachtflieger*, Hoffmann-Mainz 1966

–, Die Ritterkreuzträger der Luftwaffe-Jagdflieger, Hoffman-Mainz 1966

–, *Jagdflieger-Oberst Werner Mölders* Held, Werner Motorbuch-Stuttgart 1982

Obermaier, Ernst, *Die deutsche Luftwaffe im Afrika-Feldzug 1941-43* Held, Werner, Motorbuch-Stuttgart 1982

Priller, Josef, *JG 26 "Schlageter," Geschichte eines JG*, Motorbuch-Stuttgart 1980, 4. Aufl.

Ries, Karl, Luftwaffe Photo-Report 1919-1945, Motorbuch-Stuttgart 1984

–, *Dora Kurfürst und die rote 13*, Band I-IV, Hoffman-Mainz 1964-68

–, *Markierungen und Tarnanstriche d. Luftwaffe im 2. Weltkrieg* Band I-IV, Hoffmann-Mainz 1963-72

–, *Luftwaffenstory 1935-39*, Hoffmann-Mainz 1976

–, *Photo-Collection, Luftwaffe-Embleme*, Hoffmann-Mainz 1976

–, *Bilanz am Seitenleitwerk, Bildband*, Obermaier, Ernst Hoffmann-Mainz 1970

Rübell, Günther, *Kreuze am Himmel, wie auf Erden*, Fronterleben Orion-Heimreiter-Heusenstamm 1980

Sarowski, Heinz *Berühmte Bordfunkgeräte*, Export-Verlag 1983

Schlaug, Georg, *Die deutschen Lastensegler-Verbände 1937-45*, Motorbuch-Stuttgart 1985

Schliephake, Hanfried *Flugzeugbewaffnung*, Motorbuch-Stuttgart 1979

Schwerdtfeger, Werner *Wetterflieger in der Arktis 1940-42*, Selinger, Franz, Motorbuch-Stuttgart 1982

Sengfelder, Günter *Flugzeugfahrwerke*, Motorbuch 1979

Shores, Christopher, *Luftkampf zwischen Sand und Sonne* Ring, Hans Motorbuch-Stuttgart 1974

Shores, Christopher, *Tunesien 1942-43, Luftkämpfe über Fels und Wüste*, Ring, Hans Hess, William N., Motorbuch-Stuttgart 1981

Toliver, Raymond F., *Das waren die deutschen Jagdflieger-Asse 1939-1945*, Constable, Trevor J.

b.) Other publications

Fleuret, Alain, *Luftwaffe Camouflage & Markings*, Kookaburra-Melbourne 1981

Green, William, *Warplanes of the Third Reich*, Macdonald-London 1970

–, *War Planes of the Second World War*, Vol. 8, 9 and 10: Bombers

–, *War Planes of the Second World War*, Vol. 5 Flying Boats, Vol. 6, Floatplanes, Macdonald-London 1967

Jansen, Ab A. *Wespennest Leeuwarden*, Band I, Hollandia-Baarn (NL) 1976

–, *Sporen aan de hemel, eine Luftkriegschronik* Band I-III, Hallandia-Baarn (NL) 1979-1981

Lorant, Jean-Yves *Le Focke Wulf 190*, Frappe, Jean+B. Lariviere-Paris 1981

Merrick, K.A. *Luftwaffe Camouflage & Markings*, Vol. I, Kookaburra-Melbourne 1973

–, *The Official Monogram Painting Guide to German Aircraft 1935-1945* Hitchcock, Thomas H., Monogram Aviation Publications, Massachusetts 1980

Smith, J.R., *Luftwaffe Camouflage & Markings*, Vol. 2 1976, Vol.3 1977, Kookaburra-Melbourne
Smith, J.R., *The Modellers Luftwaffe Painting Guide*, Pentland, G.G. Kookaburra-Melbourne 1979
Lutz, R.P., Hitchcock, Thomas A. *Messerschmitt "O-Nine" Gallery*, Monogram Aviation-Boylston USA 1973
Beaman Jr., John R., *The Last of the Eagles*, Eigenverlag-Greensboro USA 1976

c.) Periodicals

Foto Archiv, Band I-IX, 1976-1982, Alba-Verlag, Düsseldorf
I.P.M.S. Deutschland Jahrgang 1976-1985, Vorstand Günther Lindow Berlin
I.P.M.S. Panorama-Österreich Jahrgang 1975-1985, Prf. Mag. Wilhelm Hesz
Jägerblatt, Jahrgang 1963-1985, Das offizielle Organ der Gemeinschaft der Jagdflieger e.V.
Luftfahrt International Band I-27, 1974-1978, Publizistisches Archiv Abt. Luftfahrt Karl R. Pawlas-Nürnberg
Luftfahrt International Jahrgang 1978-1984 E.S. Mittler & Sohn-Herford
Modell Fan Jahrgang 1974-1984, Carl Schünemann Verlag-Bremen, Redakteure Herrmann P. Dorner & Alfred W. Krüger
Plastik Modell Jahrgang 1970-1974, G. Schmidt-Verlag-Stuttgart, Chefredakteur Heinz Birkholz

d.) Original documents

A multitude of logbooks, combat/performance reports, pay books, military identification cards and other important documents from private sources.

CHAPTER 1

Luftwaffe's Pilot Training Schools

Below are listed all pilot training schools and their temporary location as known to us. As the schools frequently had to be shifted from one position to another during the course of the war, it is sometimes quite difficult to track down the exact history of a particular school. The following compilation will be updated and extended continuously.

A/B 1	Görlitz, später A 1	C9	Altenburg
C1	Sorau	B15	Bourges
B1	Schweinfurt	C16	Burg Bei Magdeburg, später B 16
A/B 2	Lexeuil	C17	Pütnitz, später B 17
C2	Neuruppen, später B 2	C18	Lüben, später B 18
A2	Straßburg	C19	Ohlau, später B 19
A/B 3	Guben, später A 3	C20	Rosenborn-Zopten, später B 20
C3	Alt-Lönewitz/Prag-Letnany, später B 2	A/B 21	Magdeburg-Ost/Deblin-Irena
		B21	Königsberg-Devau, Bialystok
A/B 4	Neudorf-Oppein/Wien-Schwechat, später A 4	C21	Bialvstok
		A/B 22	Neustadt-Giewe
C4	Sprottau, später B 4	C22	Oels, später B 22
A/B 5	Seerappen	A/B 23	Kaufberen, später
A5	Gablingen	A/B 24	Ölmütz, Kitzingen, wird mit A/B 121 Doppelschule A 121
C5	Neubrandenburg, später B 5		
A/B 6	Danzig-Langenfuhr wird A/B 52	A/B 31	Posen
C6	Kolberg, später B 6	B31	Brandis-Waldpolenz ex BFS !
A/B 7	Plauen	A/B 32	Pardublitz wird A 32, wird mit A/B 9, Doppelschule A 9
A7	Schweinfurt		
C7	Finsterwalde, Gardemoen, Radom	B32	Brünn
B7	Clermont-Ferrand, Gablingen	A/B 33	Quakenbrück, Altenburg wird BFS 10
A/B 8	Marienbad	B33	Prag-Rusin, ex BFS 3
C8	Wiener Neustadt, später B 8	B34	Kopenhagen, ex BFS 4
A/B 9	Grottkau, später A 9	B35	Milec/Polen, Hagenow-Land ex BFS 5
C9	Altenburg		
B9	Pretsch/Elbe	B36	Wesendorf ex BFS 6
A/B 10	Warnemünde, später A 10	B37	Radom, Braunschweig-Waggum ex
C10	Fürstenwalde, später B 10	BFS 7	
A/B 11	Schönwalde wird mit A/B 125 Doppelschule A 125	B38	Terespol/Seerappen ex BFS 8
		A/B 41	Frankfurt-Oder, wird A 41
C11	Zeltweg/Steiermark, später B 11	A/B 42	Prenziau/Ückermark, Neustadt - Glewe, Langensalza
A/B 12	Halberstadt/Stargard/Königsberg-Neumark		
		A42	Helmstedt
A12	Prenziau/Ückermark	A/B 43	Crailsheim wird mit A/B 124 Doppelschule A 43
C12	Prag-Rusin		
B12	Olmültz	A/B 51	Elbing, Heiligenbeil wird C 1
A/B 13	Pilsen/Neubiberg	A/B 52	Halberstadt, Danzig-Langfuhr
C13	Rosenborn-Zopten, Roth/Nümberg	A52	Danzig-Langenfuhr, Celle
B13	Roth/Nümberg	A/B 53	Plattling wird A/B 5
A/B 14	Klagenfurt, später A 1	A/B 61	Oschatz wird A 61
C14	Prag-Gbell, später B 14	A61	Werder-Oschatz

A/B 62	Bad Vöslau	
A/B 63	Marienbad/Eger	
A/B 71	Prossnitz/Sorau wird mit A/B 12 Doppelschule A 12	
A/B 72	Markersdorf-St. Pölten wird A 72	
A/B 82	Cottbus, Pretsch	
A/B 110	Stubendorf wird BFS 11	
A/B 111	Oels, Roth wird C13	
A/B 112	Langenlebarn-Tulin/Böblingen/ Inglostadt, wird LKS7	
A112	Nellingen	
A/B 113	Brünn wird mit A 3 Doppelschule A 121	
A/B 114	Zwölfaxing-Wien/Weimar-Nohra wird A 114	
A/B 115	Wels wird A 115	
A/B 116	Göppingen/Neudorf-Oppelin	
A/B 117	Bad Aibling/Kamenz	
A/B 118	Stettin-Altdamm wird A 118 Braunschweig-Broitzen	
A/B 119	Jûterbog/Damm/Kassel-Rothwesten	
A/B 120	Prenzlau/Überkmark wird A/B 2	
A/B 121	Straubing wird mit A/B 24 Doppelschule A121	
A/B 122	Jena/Gütenfeld	
A/B 123	Agram/Graz-Thalerhof wird A 123	
A/B 124	Deblin-Irena/Metz-Frescaty, Metz-Diedenhofen wird mit A/B 43 Doppelschule A 43	
A/B 125	Neukuhren wird A 125	
A/B 126	Gotha	

Air Combat Schools (Luftkriegsschulen)
1   Dresden/Klotzsche
2   Berlin/Gatow
3   Wildpark/Werder
4   Fürstenfeldbruck
5   Breslau/schöngarten
6   Kitzingen
7   Tulin
8   Göppingen
9   Tschenstochau
10   Fürstenwalde/Spree
11   Straubing
12   Bug/Rügen
13   Halle/Saale

Initial Fighter Training (Jagdfliegergervorschulen)
1   Kamenz/Sachsen
2   Lachen-Speyerdorf

3   Wien, Schwechart, Neubiberg
4   Fürth
5   Wien-Schwechat

Fighter Schools (Jagdfliegerschulen)
1   Werneuchen
2   Magdeburg, Zerbst, Schleissheim
3   Stolp-Reitz, Grove, Bad Aibling
4   Fürth/Roth
5   Wien-Schwechat, Villa Coublay, Gyancourt
6   Lachen-Speyerdorf, Eichborn

Fighter Schools, as from Spring 1943
JG 101   Werneuchen, Pau, Schongau
JG 102   Zerbst, Stolp-Reitz
JG 103   Bad Aibling, Chaneauroux, Stolp-Reitz, Pütnitz
JG 104   Fürth/Roth
JG 105   Villa Coublay-Nord, Chartres, Bourges, Gyancourt, Markersdorf
JG 106   Lachen-Speyerdorf, Reichenbach
JG 107   Nancy, Tapolca, Steinamanger, Markersdorf
JG 108   Bad Vöslau/Stuhlweissenberg (Börgend), Wiener Neustadt
JG 109   Stolp-Reitz
JG 110   Altenburg, Graz, Swinemünde

Air Force Communication Schools (Luftflottennachrichtenschulen)
1   Nordhausen
2   Königsgrätz
3   Pocking, Gablingen, München-Riem
4   Budweis, Deutsch-Brod, Lyon
5   Erfurt
6   Dievnow/Land/See

Blind-Flying Schools (Blindflugschulen)
1   Brandis, Brandis-Waldpolenz
2   Neuburg-Donau, Stargard
3   Königsberg-Devau, Enzheim, Grieslinen,
      Prag-Rusin
4   Wien-Aspern, Kopenhagen-Kastrup
5   Stargard/Belgrad-Semlin/Rahmel-Putzig
6   Celle-Wietzenbruch, Wesendorf
7   Radom/Gardemoen/Isttterburg
8   Stargard/Terespol
9   Kaunas/Litauen
10   Altenburg Wird JG 110
11   Stubendorf Wird SG 111

Radio Operator Schools (Bordfunkerschulen)
Halle/Saale

Other Schools

Aircrew Check-OutUnit
      (Flugzeugführerüberprüfungsschule)
      LF Prenzlau/Pasewalk/Salzwedel

Flying Instructor School (Fluglehrerschule der
      Luftwaffe)
Brandenburg-Briest

Night Fighter School (Nachjagdschule)
1   Schleissheim
Nachtjagdschule Neubiberg
2   Stuttgart-Echterdigen
NJG 101 Manching B. Ingolstadt vor, Schleissheim,
      München-Riem
NJG 102 Kitzingen, Powanden, Oels, Prag-Obell

Air Reconnaissance School (Aufklärerschule)
1   Grossenhain/Sachsen
2   Brieg
3   Jüterbog

Heavy Fighter School (Zerstörerschule)
1   Schleissheim
2   Memmingen, Später AG 101 Memmingen

Main Bomber Schools (Grosse Kampfliegerschule)
1   Tutow
2   Fassberg Hörsching-Linz
3   Lechfeld, Warschau-Okecie, Barth, Greifswald
4   Thorn
5   Parow B. Stralsund

Dive Bomber Initial Training (Stuka Vorschule)
1   Bad Aibling
2   Graz
3   San Damiano

Stuka Schule (Stuka Schule)
1   Kitzingen, Wertheim
2   Graz-Thalerhof, Piacenca

Ground Assault School (Schulschlachtgeschwader)

SG 101   Reims, Wischau, Alborg-West, Paris-Orly, Brünn
SG 102   Paris-Orly, Agram, Deutsch-Brod
SG 103   Metz, Lyon, Fassberg
SG 104   Tutow, Alborgg-West
SG 108   Ex JG 108
SG 111   Ex BFS 11 Stubendorf/OS Ludwigslust
SG 151   Agram, Grove
SG 152   Deblin-Irena
Ergänzungskampfgruppe 2 Quedlinburg

Glider flying with the training glider SG 38 of the Luftwaffe Gliding School on the Annaberg in Steinberg near Niederellguth. The SG 38 was the most widely used glider for basic training in the 1930s and 1940s.

"Grunau Baby" glider landing at a satellite airfield on the Annaberg in Steinberg near Niederellguth. The emblem shows a huge furnace fronted by a propeller. The actual furnace was situated near the airfield in Schlesien.

A rare sight at the Luftwaffe's Pilot Training Schools was the Arado 79. Designed as a sportive two-seater with an early retractable undercarriage, it won several air-races before the war. Considering the date of conception, this aircraft was very advanced. The picture shows a GA+?? of the Luftwaffe's flying instructor school in Brandenburg-Briest. Here the future flying instructors were given final grooming for their ever-demanding task. The Brandenburg Eagle became the school's emblem.

At the flying instructor school in Brandenburg-Briest these rather ancient Bf 109Ds spent the end of their service career. The aircraft in the foreground, WNr. 1822, carries a "Yellow 2" together with its code letters CO+ND. This "Yellow 2" may very well have stemmed from its previous unit, whereas the code letters were allocated upon arrival to the school.

Solo flight by a pupil of the A/B-1 school in Gölitz. He is flying a grey Klemm 35 with the code letters FI+FU. In the summer of 1944, this aircraft was in use with combination training school A 121 in Straubing. How this Klemm had been transferred from Görlitz to Straubing, however, is still unknown. The red triangle painted on the engine cowling states, "Attention. Do not walk here!"

At the end of 1939, this Klemm 35B, WI-ECE, belonged to the A/B-1 school in Görlitz. The rather striking color scheme was normally only applied to display aircraft. Regrettably, further details as to its origin, remain a mystery. It is only known for certain that the Klemm 35 did not possess the aerobatic qualities of a Fw 44 and was thus not assigned to any demonstration units.

On this Bücker 131, also stationed at the A/B-1 school in Gölitz, both the "Attention" emblem and the school badge were applied by spray painting. The school badge depicts a stylized aircrew. Just aft of the engine cover the WNr. 379 is still visible.

Student pilot "Jupp" Röhling taxies out in spring 1940 in an Arado 76, KQ+AU, for take-off from the training Airfield Freiwaldau of A/B 1 in Gölitz.

A rare Luftwaffe aircraft was the Czech-built Avia FL 3, a particularly small machine. Here flying instructor Fw. Breitkreuz delicately climbs aboard. The photograph was taken in 1943 or 1944. It is uncertain whether the emblem shown here actually belonged to the training school in Guben or not.

The "Nuremberg Funnel" was the emblem of FFS A/4 in Neudorf/Oppeln/Oberschlesien. Originally situated in Nuremberg, the school was transferred at the outbreak of war initially to Prag-Gbell, from where it later moved to Vienna-Schwechat until its final residence at Neudorf.

On its nose a Fw 58C shows the emblem of FFS A/B 6 Danzig Langfurth which had its training airfield in Praust and Streblin. The multi-
colored emblem reflects the city herald of Danzig.

The blind-folded cow, a motif stemming from a popular German children's game, was a frequently used emblem with the blind flying schools of the Luftwaffe. This example was photographed on a He 111 of blind flying school 7. In the center of the cow's body the outline of Scandinavia can clearly be seen. From November 1940 to April 1941 the school was based in Insterburg. In May 1941 it was transferred to Gadermoen, Norway from where the emblem possibly originated. In October 1942 the school finally moved to Radom.

The emblem of blind flying school 8 in Stargard, Pommern, temporarily also located in Terespol, not only featured the traditional "blind cow", but also a stylized griffin.

As a tribute to their origins, FFS 8 Wiener Neustadt adopted the city herald of Fürth, a clover leaf, as their unit's emblem. Training pilots Kasper and Winfried Kaiser (left to right), are standing in front of a training Ju 88A. Its port engine is completely covered by a tarpaulin.

In 1939, pilot Richard Franz trained at A/B 4 in Klagenfurt. The school's emblem, a design of two different heralds, is clearly visible on an Arado 66. Its three stylized lions in the left half are complemented by red and white stripes, possibly a reference to Kärnten, Austria.

By its emblem, an edelweiss above a mountain goat standing on a stylized range of mountains, FFS C 11 (B 11) Zeltweg/Steiermark emphasizes its alpine character.

A Ju 86G in Prag Gbell in an appalling condition. On its nose the aircraft, code ??+BR, carries the school's emblem, a raven in a yellow ring, and the letter "C" indicating the type of school. This photo was taken in 1942/43.

A very popular aircraft with C-schools was the Siebel 204D. Like the Heinkel He 111, the all-clear nose section provided ideal visibility for the pilots. Known for its versatility, the Siebel 204 was once used as an improvised night fighter and as a test plane for radio tracking. This photo shows ?N+SY of FFS C 14 Prag Gbell in summer 1943. Its registration code is rather interesting: The initially plain white letter were later replaced by black characters with a white rim. Formation flying training with Ju 86Es at FFS C 16 at Burg near Magdeburg in the winter of 1942/43. Formation flying was as rigidly instilled as parade ground drill.

This old lady, an Arado Ar 68F, joined pilot training school FAR 24 Olmütz in spring 1940 to serve out her last days. The photograph, taken at the school's airfield in Perrau, emphasizes the Arado's monstrous exhaust. Its long exhaust pipes appear to have formerly belonged to a Heinkel He 45 – at least the similarity is striking. The Arado AR 68 F formed part of the so-called "K-types" (Kampftypen) which in each school were used to prepare the pilots for the fast fighter aircraft later to be flown in frontline service.

In 1944, just prior to the flight of this Ha 139, a former mail plane, Helmut Körner, Peter Pörksen and Reinwald had this final photo taken. The flight, beginning in Pütnitz, concluded in Nordenham where the aircraft was struck off the register. Of the three planes ever built two were used by Lufthansa in the South Atlantic area. At that time, "Nordwing" carried the registration code D-AJEY. After several changes it finally joined FFS B 17 Pütnitz. The school's badge can be clearly seen below the cockpit canopy.

An essential part of a pilot's equipment was the standard seat parachute. In winter 1940/41 it was worn by flying instructor Fw. Hoffman who is depicted here standing on the wing root of his Arado AR 96 B which belonged to FFS A/B 24 in Olmütz. The automatic adjustable Argus-airscrew, propelled by a 465 hp Argus AS 410 engine, is clearly shown.

Parked at the Pardubitz/Chrudin airfield, home of A/B 32 school, was in summer 1941 is this Heinkel He 45, WNr. 337 PF+QB, of A/B 24 Olmütz. The school's emblem depicts an eagle surrounded by a circle. Interestingly, the Heinkel displays an unusual feature for a training aircraft – a yellow band around its nose. After the transfer from Kitzingen to Straubing in 1943, the school received its new name "Flugzeugführerdoppelschule A 121." This name was adapted from the A/B 24 and A 1 B 121 schools from Straubing.

Another aircraft of A/B 24 Olmütz parked in Chrudin airfield in the summer of 1941 was this Fw 56 "Stösser", PM+AP, WNr. 914. The machine also possesses the yellow band around the nose and the school's emblem. The significance of the second emblem directly forward of the code is unknown. It features a herald in two colors divided into quarters.

This Albatros AL 101, powered by a 100 hp Argus AS 8a engine, can best be described as an "airborne tortoise." This photo was taken in summer 1941 at the Braunsberg airfield of A/B Heiligenbeil, East Prussia.

This Hs 123A and Bf 108 belonged to A/B 13 Neibiberg. These photos were probably taken in 1940 in Pilsen, where the school was transferred in 1939. The meaning of the circled L which was painted on both aircraft is unknown.

In 1941, this Arado Ar 68E, VB+NQ, WNr. 1558, served with A/B 32 Pardubitz. As the Arado 68 had been a frontline fighter in the Luftwaffe's early days, it was ideal for fighter pilot training at Chrudin airfield. The significance of the white circle marking just forward of the cockpit door is unknown.

Preparing for take-off in spring 1941 at A/B 32 Pardubitz. Besides Pardubitz, the school used the Chrudin and Sbraslavice airfields. In this photograph, group flying instructor Ofw. Böhm, standing next to a Henschel He 72B, DD+G?, WNr. 445, gives final instructions to trainee pilot Uffz. Simonsohn. The front cockpit is occupied by Fw. Lindner. With the exception of a Go 145, The pupils always sat behind the instructor. Interestingly, this aircraft is equipped with skis instead of wheels.

A silhouetted white horse on a red shield was both the emblem of the town of Pardubitz, and A/B 32 pilot training school which was located there. Various stylized versions were used, the one shown here on a Heinkel He 72 prior to take-off from Pardubitz airfield being the most frequent. Powered by a 150 hp Argus AS R in-line engine, the He 72A was only built in small numbers.

FFS A/B 5 at Seerappen (black sea horse) gave an illustrated translation of the school's location by its emblem – a sea horse. The school retained its telling name even when transferred to Quakenbrück where it was redesignated and became A/B 33 in March 1941. Here, the emblem is seen on a Bücker 181, one of the Luftwaffe's more modern aircraft at the time. Eventually, this aircraft replaced the Fw 44 and the He 72 in flight training. Noteworthy is the fully enclosed canopy, fitted with large forward opening panels. The netting behind the crew served as separation to the baggage area.

In Luftwaffe service, the Ju 52/3m was a true workhorse, and thus was found with nearly all units. At FFS B 34 in Copenhagen/Kastrup this Ju 52, carrying the white-bordered registration code VK+AZ, was used for blind-flying training in 1943/44. The parallel yellow bands running around the center of the fuselage confirm this role.

Originally developed as a commercial airliner, this He 111G-3 was used for blind-flying training at FFS B 34 in Copenhagen in 1943/44. In contrast to all previous versions, this aircraft featured two BMW 132H radial engines of 880 hp each which were designed for rapid replacement (the engine including the cowling could be replaced as one unit). Here also the registration code CE+NX is bordered in white.

A trainee pilot entering an Ar 66 of FFS A/B 62 in Bad Vöslau. The school's emblem existed in two forms: The ornate version shown here contrasted strongly with the plain square version.

Formation flying with the faithful Fw 44 at A/B 71 Prossnitz/Mähren in 1941. The formation entering a turn to port thus allows the viewer to glimpse at the frozen March River in Mähren.

On February 11, 1942 teacher pilot Helmut Buntje was making a landing approach with the student pilot Seidelmann in a Bü 131 in Prossnitz and rammed another Bücker just before touchdown. To the left is DK+GB with a normal undercarriage and on the right is ??+IZ with skis from the A/B 71 in Prossnitz. Skis could be mounted without difficulty instead of the normal undercarriage. However, it was not in general use at all schools in winter.

Driving through the air in an open two-seater, even if it is only practicing formation flying with the Klemm 35D, is shown here in the year 1941 at the A/B 71 in Prossnitz. However, the pilots Görlitz and Freund seem to like it. The Klemm had been designated as an aerobatic sports and touring plane. Many pilots made their first hops with Kl 35s.

This photo shows some irregularities. According to the owner of the photo and the entries in his pay book this Kl 35B belongs to the A/B 72 Markersdorf/St. Polten, Austria. The emblem on the fuselage is the school's symbol, at least in the time accounted for from July 17, 1940 to June 10, 1941. According to a different source, the school's emblem consisted of an abstract plane over a snow-covered hilltop. Of course, the school may have changed its emblem at some time.

Two different symbols were used as school emblems at the FFS A/B 113 in Brünn. On this Bücker 131 DA+RR the so-called "Detmold swimming trunks" are visible, a sign referring to the original base of the school in Detmold. In October 1939, the school was transferred to Brünn and kept its emblem. This formation flying picture was taken during 1940. The Bücker 131 was considered to be a well-thought-out design. The aircraft was fully aerobatic and was only surpassed by the Bü 133 in popularity. Quite a few aerobatics contests were won with it.

This photo of a He 72 on skis was taken at A/B 113 in Brünn in the winter 1941/42. A student pilot is preparing for his solo flight. The exhaust fumes from the seven cylinder engine were collected in an exhaust collector ring and fed into this pipe. The pilot did not have to suffer from the exhaust and the ring functioned as a silencer at the same time.

We can clearly see the second version of the school's emblem of the A/B 113 in Brünn. It shows the "Herrmannsdenkmal" (Statue of Arminius the Cheruskan) and was used along with the "Detmold swimming trunks" emblem within the school. It is unknown why two emblems were used. Flying instructor Heberer is preparing for the next training flight in 1942. Note the opened hatch.

A Flying student before his next flight in the Kl 35 at the FFS (Flugführerschule) A/B 114 in Vienna-Zwölfaxing. The instructors seat was in the front and the pupil's seat was in the back in the Klemm 35. The school's emblem at the A/B 114 was a flying eagle in a shield.

Pupil Walter Reinicke has crashed his Gotha 145A on the airfield of A/B 115 in Wels, Ansbach. Unfortunately we cannot determined the exact moment of the crash landing. This school's emblem, a catfish (in German: Wels) on a shield, can be seen clearly on the fuselage between the wings of the DF+IF.

The flying schools received a very versatile aircraft in the Arado 96B. This photo shows DL+?? with flying instructor Willi Deutsch (in the front seat) during blind flying practice at FFS A/B 115 Wels. We can see that the rear part of the canopy is covered to permit the pupil no view of the outside during blind flying. Of course, there was no formation flying during such practice flights. The "catfish emblem" is clearly visible below the cockpit.

The Arado 96B may have belonged to the FFS A/B 119 Kassel Rothwesten, but this was not necessarily a school's emblem, as the school is known to have had an emblem with a pupil riding on a bird within a round shield with the inscription A/B 119. The aircraft, however, also may have belonged to the Luftwaffe pilot's school, training command Quedlinburg (accounted for by the log for the period from July 2, 1943 to August 1, 1944).

Student pilots Walner and Müller on the Lucho base of FFS A/B 123 (Croatian) in Agram are standing ready for a souvenir photo in March 1943. The school's emblem is painted on the fuselage to the left of the exhaust. Note the landing light under the left wing of the Go 145. This type of aircraft was also used for twilight flights.

A Klemm 31A XIV or a Kl 32B XIV? The two aircraft are practically identical in their outer appearance. In contrast to the three-seat Kl 32, which had flaps as additional equipment in the same wing structure, the Kl 31 was a four-seater. BB+XG belonged to the Fliegerausbildungsregiment (pilot's training regiment) 28 in Völkenrode. The center section of the fuselage had been resprayed, when the sports plane received the unit markings instead of the civilian D-markings.

It is not clear which school this Arado 66 belongs to. A raven or similar bird carrying a control column under its right wing can be seen on the emblem. Because of this we believe that this plane belongs to a flying school. The number of unknown emblems still appearing is quite astonishing.

A flight simulator, the so-called Link Trainer. The pupil was taught the feeling of flying without using any fuel or endangering lives. Today the flight simulator is major part of pilot training.

This plane too is supposed to have flown! A post-office clerk from Düsseldorf built this little aircraft himself in 1936. It was the only one built, yet there is no evidence of it having been used in the pilots schools.

In this photograph two members of the ground crew crank the starting handle of a Junkers W 34 hau. In the late summer of 1939 the aircraft carried the emblem of the LKS 1 in Dresden-Klotzsche on the engine cowling. It depicts a sword with wings and the inscription "LKS Dresden."

This photo of an Ar 96B, DC+?? from the LKS 3 Wildpark-Werder was taken in September or October 1943. The emblem in front of the WNr. 1108 shows a park landscape with a lake and flowers. The position of the WNr. below the cockpit canopy of the plane is unusual.

November 20, 1940 at the LKS 4 in Fürstenfeldbruck. Flying pupil Meiss is standing on a Junkers W 34 from the Luftkriegsschule in position for a souvenir photo. The meaning of the elk on the aircraft is not known yet. Most likely it was not the school's emblem.

This photo shows an Ar 96B "25" from the Jagdfliegervorschule 2 (Fighter pilot's preparatory training school) in Lachen-Speyerdorf. The emblem is not clearly recognizable but definitely identical to the one on the next photograph, with one little but important difference: The lower right hand quarter contains a Roman II, which could mean the JFVS 2. This however, cannot be proven with certainty.

This Ar 96B "84" belongs to the Jagdfliegervorschule 3 in Vienna-Schwechat; we can clearly recognize the symbol. On the upper left hand side the letter JV = Jagdfliegervorschule and at the bottom on the right a Roman III = the third JFVS. It may be assumed that all JFVS had the same symbol and only the inscription in Roman numbers was consecutive. The fighter pilot training schools also all had the same symbol, which only varied or received additions within the schools. In the aircraft is Gefr. Norbert Feser.

The story behind this nose-up of a Heinkel 51 "43" is not clear. According to the flight-log of Rudi Dannat, the owner of this photograph, the aircraft could only belong to the "Jagdfliegerschule" (Fighter School) in Schleissheim. Rudi Dannat was there as a trainee between August, 1939 and October 15, 1939. Among others, he flew the He 51. But could there have been snow in Schleissheim by mid-October? Dannat was then transferred to I./Ergänzungstaffel JG 2 (replacement squadron), where he flew the Bf 109 exclusively. Note that the registration is also shown on the upper wing, in the style of the pre-war fighter markings.

Uffz. Zeiser (?) with his Bf 109E of "Jagdfliegerschule 2" at Zerbst/Anhalt in either autumn 1941 or spring 1942. The school's emblem shown below the canopy, consists of the fighter's emblem, a winged arrow, and "Jagdfl. Schule 2" written above.

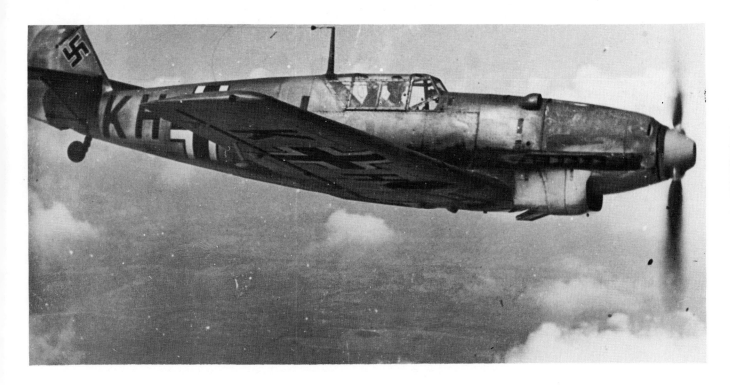

The fighter schools used those aircraft that had been phased out of front line combat units, like this Bf 109D, KH+??, with its coolant outlet half open. This photo was taken at "Jagdfliegerschule 3"/Bad Aibling in late summer 1942. The fighter schools frequently changed their location, which makes it somewhat difficult to relate the fields to one school. In 1940, JFS 3 (fighter school) was based in Stolp/Reitz.

This nearly camouflaged Bf 109E had supposedly been in use at the front, where this camouflage scheme was customary. In late summer 1941 it arrived in Liegescourt, France, 1./JFS 5. Sixteen victory bars on the rudder show the Gruppenkommandeur's kills. We assume that this Bf 109E had belonged to II./JG 54 and came to I./JFS 5 after having been rebuilt to Bf 109F standard, as shown here. Accordingly, it is not the aircraft of the commander of I./JFS 5, but just one of the unit's many Bf 109s.

This Bf 109D "Black 17", with white streaks behind its tail. The photograph was probably taken in summer 1940 at III./JFS 5, Vienna-Schwechat. The school was later transferred to Tousse le Noble.

On August 26, 1944, flight instructor Christian Alt made a forced landing in a Bf 109G-12 of I./JG 106. The Bf 109G-12 was intended to make the trainees familiar with a faster type than the Ar 96. As the Bf 109 was very difficult to handle, there were many crashes, especially during the first training flights. The Bf 109G-12 was fitted with a larger cabin and dual controls to be used as a fighter trainer. However, the fuselage tank had to be removed, which restricted the aircraft's range.

Formation flight with I./JG 106 in 1944/45 in Baltringen. The Ar 96 B's bear their unit markings on the fuselage as well as a provisional number, here "256." In March, 1943 the "Jagdfliegerschulen" were renamed as "Jagdgeschwader" (Fighter Squadrons). JFS 1 became "Jagdgeschwader 101", and JFS 2, "JG 102."

A roll and dive to the left, 3./JG 106 in August, 1944. At this time, I./JG 106 was based in Schussenried. These Ar 96Bs, too, feature a number code besides their ordinary markings. Here the number is "278", this time however, properly painted.

Emil Schierling as a fighter trainee in July 1944 in Steinamanger, Hungary in front of his Bf 109G of JG 107. Interestingly, the "11" is not painted beside the Balkenkreuz, but is shown in small numbers ahead of the supercharger intake. Note the improved visibility "Erla" canopy and wing gondolas for the MG 151/20 guns.

This unusually painted Bf 109G was seen in summer 1944 with JG 107 in Steinamanger, Hungary. Quite unusual is the shape of the "13" and the fuming bull in a circle beneath the canopy. The aircraft was mainly used in taxiing exercises with trainees.

In April, 1941, the EJG 51 transferred from La Rochelle to Krakow, Poland, changing their name to "Jagdergänzungsgruppe Ost" (Fighter replacement Group East). The engine cowling of this Bf 109E displays this unit's emblem, a diving Bf 109.

The concrete apron at Krakow, too, belongs to "J.Gr.Ost." Here, the trainees received their final training before being transferred to the combat units.

Marseille-Mariagne in autumn 1943, then the base of "J.Gr.Süd" (Fighter Replacement Group South). The aircraft of this unit feature various camouflage schemes.

Among others, some Bf 109Gs were in use with J.Gr.Süd in Marseille-Mariagne in autumn 1943. They feature two 20mm MG 151/20s in underwing gondolas as additional armament against four-engine bombers. There is an emblem ahead of the supercharger intake: an eagle, feeding its brood. In literature, the emblem is usually related to EJG 1, as unit emblem or to J.Gr.Süd. However, neither is the case here. Its affiliation still remains unknown.

Henri Thiedemann as a pilot in front of his Fw 190A of J.Gr.West in August/September 1944 in Märkisch-Friedland. The painting beneath the canopy is the personal emblem of flight instructor Franz Steiner.

This photo was taken in August/September 1944 at J.Gr.West in Märkisch-Friedland. It shows Franz Steiner's Fw 190A. As no one wanted to fly the "13" he took it over as a fighter instructor. Note the removed or folded back engine cowlings. In front of the aircraft "Hein" Umland, Franz Steiner and Rechter can be seen (from left to right).

The coat of arms on this Ar 96B definitely belongs to a still unknown fighter-pilot school. Unfortunately the photographer died before we received this photo. On the left hand side of the coat of arms in a rectangle with the inscription "Kaltstart" (cold weather starting).

Nothing is known about the coat of arms on this Ar 96B. It shows a top hat on a stick in an escutcheon. We believe that this photo was taken in a fighter-pilot school.

This carved owl was the squadron symbol of 1./Nachtjagdschule 1 in Schleissheim in 1942. We were not able to discover whether this sign was also used on the aircraft.

Amongst several Ar 96s and Bf 110s was a Bf 108B liaison aircraft at the Zerstörerschule 2 in Memmingen in winter 1942/43. The school's coat of arms was painted on the fuselage of CP+??.

This Ju 88G belonged to Luftnachrichtenschule 6 (See) Dievenow/Wollin. The G-type was developed from the E-type used with and was used by the Luftwaffe in large quantities. It only differed from the E-type by an enlarged fully-glazed nose. To the left of the "2", the coat of arms of the school can be seen after it had been adapted to suit the mission area over the Baltic. It is a bundle of lightning flashes over the waves of the sea.

Landing approach of a Ju W 34 hi, T3+NX of Bordfunkerschule Halle/Salle in 1940. On the engine cowling is the school's coat of arms. Not the directional loop aerial and aerial mast on the upper side of the fuselage. The bay for the training aerial is located on the underside of the fuselage.

One might think this Ju 87D belonged to I./St.G.1. This is indeed an aircraft from this unit with the raven design emblem, but after it had been transferred to I./SG 101. This photo was taken between May and August 1944 in Wischau, Moravia. Ulrich Horn, in front of the aircraft in which he had learned combat flying. Interesting features are the dive brakes, the barrel of the MG 151/20 and the drop tank under the starboard wing.

This Bü 181, RK+JL flies over a small town, probably in East Prussia. The flying school it belongs to is unknown, though it could be FFS A 52 Danzig-Langfuhr. The still-unknown legend St.u.K. in front of the cockpit is worth noting.

CHAPTER II

Reconnaissance Units of the Luftwaffe

Aufkl.Gr		10	
Aufkl.Geschw.			11
Aufkl.Gr.		11	
Aufkl.Geschw.			12
Aufkl.Gr.		12	
Aufkl.Geschw.			13
Aufkl.Gr.		13	
Aufkl.Gr.		14	
Aufkl.Gr.		21	
Aufkl.Gr.		22	
Aufkl.Gr.		23	
Aufkl.Gr.		31	
Aufkl.Gr.		32	
Aufkl.Gr.		33	
Aufkl.Gr.		41	
Aufkl.Gr.	(F)	120	
Aufkl.Gr.	(F)	121	
Aufkl.Gr.	(F)	122	
Aufkl.Gr.	(F)	123	
Aufkl.Gr.	(F)	124	
Aufkl.Gr.	(Nacht)		

FAG 1
FAG 2
FAG 3
FAG 4
FAG 5

NAG 1
NAG 2
NAG 3
NAG 4
NAG 5
NAG 6
NAG 7
NAG 8
NAG 9
NAG 10
NAG 11
NAG 12
NAG 13
NAG 14
NAG 15
NAG 16

Aufkl.St. Krim
III.Aufkl.Gr.LG 2

Luftbildstaffel 1

Versuchsstelle f. Höhenflüge

Aufkl.Kommando Rowehl
Aufkl.Gr.(F) Ob.d.L.
Aufkl.Gr.(F) 100
Aufkl.St. d.Gen.d.L. beim Ob.d.H.
Aufkl. Schule 1

5./ErgGr.(F) Rahmel

The list shows only the most important units.

Staff meeting in Oranienburg at the Versuchsverband des Ob.d.L. (Oberkommando der Luftwaffe/Luftwaffe high command). This photograph from 1943 shows the high altitude reconnaissance version of the Ju 86P bomber in the foreground. In the background a four-engine He 116 covered by tarpaulins is visible. The round lid in front of the feet of the two people on the left side is the seal of the pressure cabin of this Ju 86P. The round entry port of the aircraft is barely visible above the ladder.

Pilot Otto Seelig flies his Ju 86P from the Versuchsverband des Ob.d.L. over the Black Forest in 1940. The main features in comparison to the bomber version were: a great increase in span, a Jumo-207 Diesel engine with high-altitude supercharger and a pressurized cabin. With these, the aircraft was able to reach an altitude of 14,000 meters and thus could not be reached by interceptors or anti-aircraft guns.

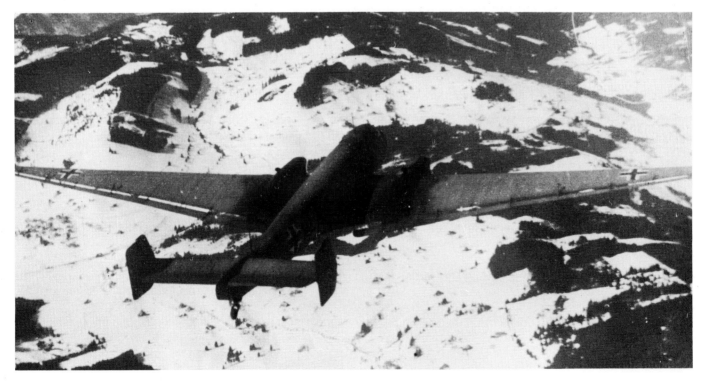

Another photo of a Ju 86P of the Versuchsverband des Ob.d.L., this time in Oranienburg in 1944. The entrance hatch is clearly recognizable. Interesting features are the four bladed propellers, the very large radiator below the diesel engine, and the large air intake of the supercharger in the leading edge.

The asymmetrical Blohm & Voss Bv 141 was a curiosity among Luftwaffe aircraft. This one was probably from the Versuchsverband des Ob.d.L. in 1944 in Grossenhain/Sachsen. Better visibility for the crew was the aim of the asymmetric configuration in this reconnaissance aircraft. The Bv 141 displayed very good flying characteristics, but it was not put into large-scale production and only a few aircraft were used on the Eastern Front for test purposes.

The reconnaissance version of the Ju 88S high speed bomber was designated Ju 88T. These photos show such an aircraft of the Ob.d.L. or of the I./Aufkl.Gr.Ob.d.L. (reconnaissance group) in Toulouse/Blagnac, France in 1944. The lower nose gun nacelle is missing on this version. The lack of armament except for one rear machine gun is noticeable. Speed was its weapon.

This Ju 188E belongs to the Versuchsverband des Ob.d.L. Where the photo of the T9+LH from 1. Staffel was taken is unfortunately unknown. The gunner's position in the top of the cabin has been removed. This was also partly done in the fighting units, in order to have faster aircraft. The black camouflage high up on the fin and rudder is also unusual. There is a 900 liter tank in a transport crate in the foreground.

Two more rare birds of the Aufkl.Gr.Ob.d.L. Here an He 116B with the markings T5+BH from 1. Staffel. Originally designed as a long-range mail plane, this aircraft suffered from the lack of powerful high-altitude engines. Finally the B-series was produced as a study for a four-engine bomber.

The Blohm & Voss Ha 142 was a long-range landplane version of the mail seaplane Ha 139B. The main differences were the under-carriage and the BMW 132 H-1 engines instead of the Jumo 205 C-Diesel engines. The photograph shows the Ha 142V-2, T5+CH of 1./Aufkl.Gr.Ob.d.L.

In the foreground a Ju 86B with the registration D-AEAF, which probably once belonged to Lufthansa. This aircraft was developed for a Lufthansa tender requirement, but was also used with little success in different versions with bomber units of the Luftwaffe. There is an He 111 in the background, T5+RH of 1./Aufkl.Gr.Ob.d.L.

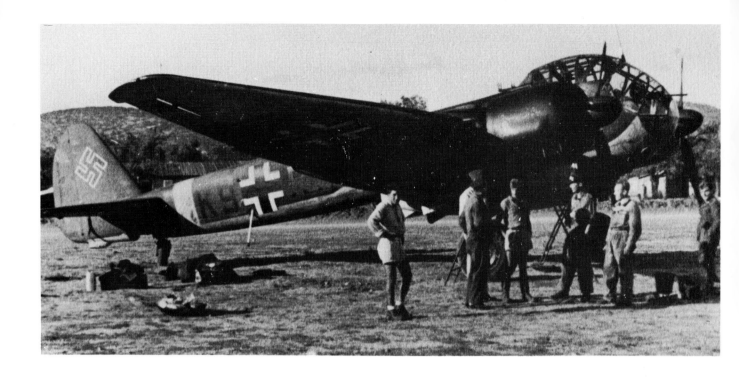

These two photos are very rare, as they show a Ju 88B-0, K9+RH of 1./Aufkl.Gr.Ob.d.L. in 1940. Only ten were built and were later developed into the Ju 88E, which finally became the Ju 188E. The Ju 88B-0 mainly differed from the A-version through an aerodynamically-improved cockpit and the BMW 801 engine instead of the Jumo 211.

A photo from the 1000th mission of the 1./(F)Ob.d.L., towards the end of 1942 in Orscha, Russia. Members of the Staffel gather in front of a Ju 88D for a photo. Unfortunately we can only recognize Staffelkapitän Hptm. Hans Schech (second from left) and Oblt. Loak (second from right) with a zero around his neck. Hptm. Schech is supposed to have become TO (technical officer) for the General of the reconnaissance squadrons.

Pilot Richard Franz has completed his 110th flight on the front and is awarded the enemy missions badge in gold. This photo was taken in spring of 1943 after his return from a reconnaissance flight over Moscow in the high altitude reconnaissance Ju 86P. A photo-map of the city was obtained during this flight. The 1.(F)/Ob.d.L. was renamed 1.(F)/100 on March 26, 1943, so it is unknown which unit Richard Franz belonged to when the photo was taken. The squadron emblem was retained for some time afterwards.

Men from the photographic unit of the 7.(F)/LG 2 are drying the latest photos taken by the aircrews in Schwinigorotga, Russia during the summer of 1941. The exposed films were developed, dried and evaluated immediately after the return from a mission in order to have a picture of the current situation as soon as possible.

In 1940 L2+FR was parked under a camouflage net near Brussels. This time the devil emblem can be seen on the port side of the fuselage. It was customary with 7.(F)/LG 2 to paint the squadron emblem onto both sides of the fuselage. Note the landing light in the leading edge in front of the Balkenkreuz.

This shot of a Bf 110C from 7.(F)/GL 2 was taken either in Rumania or Russia during the summer of 1941. The squadron emblem, a devil's head, is painted onto the nose of this aircraft. L2+?R has a distinctive mottled camouflage on the fuselage sides and engines, while the upper surfaces have a segmented camouflage. Note the white spinner tips.

Another aircraft, L2+BR, from 7.(F)/LG 2 in the summer of 1941 during a mission near Krimentschuk, Russia. Note the camouflage on the upper surfaces.

Without a doubt the strutted high-wing monoplane Henschel Hs 126A was an army reconnaissance (Heeresaufklärer) plane, and was in service from the beginning. HS+II, WNr. 3058, from 9.(H)/LG 2 is on a practice flight which had started in its home base Kosel/Upper Silesia. The narrow Balkenkreuz on the fuselage was typical for the year 1938. The sighting lines for dropping bombs, the bay for the trailing aerial and the step to the right of this bay are interesting details.

This Fw 189A stationed in Belgium in 1941 also belonged to 9.(H)/LG 2. The Focke-Wulf gradually replaced the Hs 126 in the army reconnaissance squadrons. It was considerably more modern and suited the reconnaissance requirement. Visibility for the crew was excellent due to the fully-glazed cabin. In addition, the Fw 189A was about 100km/hr faster due to its two 465 hp Argus AS 410 A-1 engines. This fact offered the crew increased safety against enemy aircraft and also groundfire.

At the beginning of the war the Hs 126A was the backbone of the German army reconnaissance units. This Hs 126A, A1+CH in the winter of 1939-1940 belongs to 1./Aufkl.Gr.12 in Mannheim. Interesting features are the partly-removed undercarriage fairings due to the snow, and the white bomb-sighting lines on the side of the fuselage. They were for 1000, 500, 100 and 50 meters; only the first two are visible on this aircraft.

The size of this Hs 126A, 4E+FK of 2./Aufkl.Gr. 13 in Böblingen 1939, is clearly visible in this photo. At first glance, the Staffel emblem seems to be an owl armed with a magnifying glass, which also corresponds to other literature. When looked at closely it is in fact the evil queen from "Snow White" with her mirror and cloak. Note the open radiator flaps around the Bramo 323 engine and the large ladder under the fuselage.

Washing day at 3.(F)/22, 1942 in Dno, Russia. A ground mechanic is wiping the window panels of a Ju 88. An interesting feature is the washed-out camouflage on the side of the aircraft's fuselage. Note the forward defensive MG 131 machine gun and its sights.

These are the rear gun positions with two MG 81 7.9mm on a Ju 88 from 3.(F)/22 in Dno 1942. The window panels of the lens-type machine gun mounts are made of armored glass.

The Cross with the diamond in the middle was the emblem of Fernaufklärerstaffel 3.(F)/22. This photograph was taken in 1942, when the squadron was stationed in Dno. Besides the Ju 88, the Staffel was also equipped with Bf 110s.

Another occasion to celebrate: The 3000th sortie of 1.(H)/31 on March 17, 1942, in Wesenburg, Estonia. The crew (from left): Fw. Weber (gunner), Ofw. Kappes (observer) and Ofw. Fox (pilot) in front of their Fw 189A. However we do not know whether the emblem above the "3000" is a squadron emblem or rather the work of a ground staff artist. It clearly shows a stylized Fw 189.

This photograph, showing the squadron emblem of 1.(H)31, was taken somewhere on the eastern front. Normally, the emblem was sprayed on the outboard side of the engines. The abbreviation "Flivo" stands for "Fliegerverbindungsoffizier" (liaison officer) and does not belong to the squadron emblem. The liaison officer's duty was to coordinate Luftwaffe and Heer (army) operations.

The refuelling of a Ju 88D or A, featuring the emblem of 1.(F)/20 in the original version, taken in 1941 in Stavanger-Sola Land. The vehicle on the left is the oxygen truck, and on the right is a tanker. The bottom side of the fuselage shows the fairings for the Rb 20/ 30 or 50/30 cameras ("Reihenbildgeräte") which were used during reconnaissance missions. Unlike the aircraft in the photo on the top of page 80, the ventral turret of this Ju 88 is not armored. As an additional defensive armament, an MG/FF 20 mm is installed in the nose. It could also be used against naval targets on "armed reconnaissance" missions.

The port engine of this Ju 88D or A of 1.(F)/120 is being test run in Norway during 1942. The coolant outlets of the Jumo 211 G engine are open. The started trailer, which was needed to start up the engines by accumulator assistance, can be seen under the aircraft.

Bardufoss, Norway, in winter 1942/43. A member of the Luftwaffe poses for a photo in front of a Ju 88D or A 1.(F)/120. Interestingly, the emblem has been painted over with an elk's antlers. Former members of the squadron believe that the emblem was too striking. Note the open, armored access hatch on the ventral gun gondola and the 900 liter belly tank under the right wing.

OPPOSITE: This "balance of success" lurked through aviation literature for many years. The tail of Ju 88, WNr. 1867, A6+HH has repeatedly been allotted to Oberst Werner Baumbach. However, the photograph was taken at Stavanger-Sola Land by a former member of 1.(F)/120, who remembers that the aircraft was mainly flown by Staffelkapitän Hauptmann Helmuth Orlowski ("Ritterkreuz" on September 19, 1943) and his observer, Oberleutnant Fritz Heidenreich ("Ritterkreuz" on June 3, 1941). The aircraft painter, whose name was Klinkohr, often had to poise his brush and add another ship's silhouette. It can be assumed from the fact that the aircraft was flown by several crews that the victories depicted are related to this particular aircraft rather than to any single person. However, this definitely is not the Ju 88 flown by Werner Baumbach.

CHAPTER III

Miscellaneous Units

This chapter gives a survey of various Luftwaffe departments. In the following, we give a list of miscellaneous Luftwaffe units, which however must be regarded as incomplete.

Wettererkundungsstaffeln
Westa 1 des OB.d.L.
Westa 2 des Ob.d.L.
Westa 1
Westa 3
Westa 6
Westa 7
Westa 26
Westa 27
Westa 51
Westa 76

Torpedowaffenplatz Gotenhafen

Erp.Kdo. Rechlin
Erp.Stelle Rechlin
Erp.Stelle Travemünde
Erp.Stelle Tarnewitz
Erp.Stelle Grossetto
Erp.Stelle Werneuchen

Luftdienstkommando 61
Luftdienstkommando 62
Luftdienstkommando 64
Luftdienstkommando 65
Luftdienstkommando 67
Luftdienstkommando 68

Feldpoststaffel Mitte
Feldpoststaffel Süd
Feldpoststaffel Nord
Flugbereitschaft Kd.Gen.d.L. in Finnland
Flugbereitschaft d. Lfl. Kdo. 1
Flugbereitschaft d. Lfl. Kdo. 2
Flugbereitschaft Norwegen
Flugbereitschaft RLM Staaken
Flugbereitschaft (San.) 7

Fliegerverbindungs Geschwader 2

Grossraumseglerkommando 2

Schleppgruppe 1-4

Fliegerzielgeschwader 2

Zielstaffel 10

Führungskette X. Fliegerkorps

Regierungsstaffel

Kurierstaffel des OKW
Kurierstaffel des Ob.d.L.
Kurierstaffel des Ob.d.H.
Kurierstaffel des Ob.d.M.
Kurierstaffel des Führers
Kurierstaffel 1-11, 13, 14, 40, A, F

Verbindungsstaffel 7, Fliegerdivision
Verbindungsstaffel zbV. 1-4
Verbindungsstaffel zbV. 51-60
Verbindungsstaffel zbV. 62, 63, 64, 67, 70
Verbindungsstaffel zbV. 65, 300, 400

Wüstennotstaffel
Sonderkommando Blaich
Überführungskommando des Chefs d.
Ausbildungswesen

This Fw 58B was flown with II./JG 51 in northern France during 1940-1941. Its main duty was to search for aircrews shot down over the Channel and to initiate their recovery. Note the grating under the fuselage. A trapdoor ahead of this grating was used to drop a life raft, supplies or other items. The grating was intended to keep the life raft clear of the generator behind. The dorsal MG 15 in its circular mount is clearly visible.

Another sea rescue aircraft, an Fw 58C, DO+JXQ. This photograph was taken in Leeuwarden in 1940, prior to its next take-off for a sea patrol flight This can be assumed since the crew member, visible in the former dorsal gun position, wears a life jacket. The aircraft is white over all and still bears the old-style Swastika in a red stripe, as well as red crosses on wings and fuselage.

This photograph shows the first Fi 156 to be delivered to the German Navy in winter 1938, on the frozen Baltic Sea. The "Storch", D-IFRX, featured the original paint scheme provided by the manufacturer: black wings, fuselage white all over with red undercarriage legs.

The famous "Fieseler Storch" also was used by the Red Cross. DE+CA is white over all, seen visiting Kassel-Rothwesten in 1942.

An Fi 156 "Storch", 4Q+PH of 1./Fliegerdivision 7, ready for take-off. The aircraft was used as a courier and liaison aircraft.

A Bf 108B of an unknown liaison unit, skillfully "dismantled" by Flugzeugführer (pilot) Siegfried Voss. Now the ground crew takes over. Note the jack beneath the aircraft.

"Flugzeugführer" W. Zeugner in his white Arado 79 KH+?? of an unknown unit. The emblem is a winged globe, probably belonging to a liaison unit. Note the rear view mirror on top of the cabin.

A Do 17E visiting the operational field of JFS 4/Fürth in Unterschlauersbach. The nose of BB+A. shows a dog, an emblem, which is unknown to us.

Running down the engines of a Do 215 ?W+?V on an airfield in the Mediterranean area. It is not clear which unit it belongs to. Probably a reconnaissance or staff transport aircraft. The mounting points in the nose do not carry any guns, but are sealed.

In 1940 this wooden dummy Ju 88 with the registration E1+A4 could be seen on the airfield Stavanger-Sola. From the air it was difficult to tell the difference between it and a real aircraft. The British were distracted from the real airfields by such dummies during air raids.

This Klemm 32B XIV was also used in the stand-by command of the Luftflottenkommando 2 (Kesselring). This shot was taken either in Trapani, Sicily or some airfield in North Africa.

Generalfeldmarschall Kesselring in the pilot's seat of his Siebel Sh 104 SG+GH. Most likely this shot was taken in the Mediterranean area.

Pilot Fw. Rudi Dannat crashed the staff aircraft of the Chief of Command South, Generalfeldmarschall Kesselring, on February 3, 1942 in Rimini during a transfer flight from Munich to Italy. In contrast to the photo before, the aircraft SG+GH has no white fuselage band yet.

For some time the general of the fighter pilots, Adolf Galland, used to go on his official flights in an Sh 104. The emblems of the units visited by him were painted on the plane. From left to right the symbols of the following units can be seen: JG 51, V.(Z)/LG 1, JG 52, JG 3, the supplementary destroyer group, later known as I./SG 152, the infantry assault badge and II./SG 1. There were more symbols painted onto the Siebel, as seen from other photographs.

The danger of being shot down became greater with the increasing presence of the allied pilots over German territory, so the general of the fighter pilots replaced his Siebel Sh 104 with a Fw 190A. At the beginning of 1944 Generalleutnant Adolf Galland visited Erprobungskommando 25, an experimental unit for testing special weapons against bombers, in Parchim under command of Horst Geyer with his Fw 190 which had the squadron commander's chevrons and a "2." Top photo right hand side Hptm. Horst Geyer, Gen. Adolf Galland stands in the cockpit. Bottom photo from right to left: Dr. Emmert, Horst Geyer, v. Kornatzki, Gen. Adolf Galland.

The He 111 shown in this photo does not belong to a normal unit but was used for making the film "Kampfgeschwader Lützow." The unofficial coat of arms of this unit was painted to the right of the cockpit. Note the balloon-type microphone above the wing.

This photo also shows an He 111 from the film "Kampfgeschwader Lützow." The unofficial coat of arms on the fuselage is clearly visible.

All types of aircraft were used in the air service units. This Junkers W 34 hi WL+OPFB "Karlheinz Künzler" was one of them. The W 34 was developed from the W 33, using the well-known corrugated-metal construction. This photo was taken in front of the air traffic control of the airfield Mannheim-Stadt (Mannheim central airport). The origin of the aircraft was also painted onto the tailplane: Luftdienstkommando Mannheim Stadt Tel. Nr. (Air service unit center of Mannheim, Telephone No.). An interesting feature is the markings in small letters behind the Balkenkreuz without black outlines. The Balkenkreuz had been sprayed over the former markings on the wing.

This is an interesting photo of a Do 17F, the GS+NR from the air service. This Dornier, already slightly battered, was used in July 1943 as a practice target for the anti-aircraft guns. This was one of the main tasks for the air service units. The red triangular air service symbol is clearly visible here.

Both photos on this page were taken on the airfield Magdeburg-East in the beginning of 1945 and show two different Mistel composite practice aircraft consisting of a Bf 109 and Ju 88 during takeoff. The pilots were to practice their missions on these composites. For these missions the nose was removed and replaced with a 3.5 ton warhead. The pilot in the Bf 109 directed the aircraft into the target run, where the directional control was activated and the upper component was released by explosive charges. The Mistelcomposites were used during the Invasion in Normandy and against bridges over the Oder.

A picture of the Ju 188E ??+PG in Kamenz/Saxony. As this photo was taken from the front, we can read the inscription on the propeller blades: "Erprobung, Ausbesserung verboten (Experimental), do not repair)." Standing in front of their aircraft from left to right: Richard Dahm, John and Zitzmann.

A Ju 88S-3 was also used at the Erprobungsstelle der deutschen Luftfahrtindustrie (EDL) (Experimental unit of the German aircraft industry) in Kamenz/Saxony in 1944. It was used for the evaluation of a wooden propeller with extra wide blades. These blades also carry the inscription "Erprobung, Ausbesserung verboten." Note the opened floor hatch of the aircraft. In front, from left to right flight mechanic Paul Weise, chief pilot Richard Dahm and Armin Beer.

Testpilot Richard Dahm and his "Thunderbuck", a Fw 190A with oversized airscrew and a new variable-pitch system. This photo was taken by EDL at the Schwarz-Propeller factory.

To define this version of the Bf 108 is somewhat difficult. Contrary to the "normal" Bf 108B, this one is equipped with an automatic Argus variable-pitch propeller as used with the "C" version of the Bf 108, of which only a few were built. But there were also Bf 108Bs with variable-pitch airscrews. A further difference between the "A" and "B" versions was the engine. The "B" with a 240 HP Argus As-10 and the "C" with the 400 HP Hirth HM-512. This photo was taken some time in the summer of 1944 in France at an unknown unit.

Chapter IV

FIGHTER UNITS

Following is a list of the most important fighter units.

JG 1 Oesau
JG 2 Richthofen
JG 3 Udet
JG 4
JG 5 Eismeer
JG 6 Horst Wessel
JG 7
JG 10
JG 11
JG 20
JG 21

JGr 25
JG 26 Schlageter
JG 27
JG 44
JGr 50
JG 51 Mölders
JG 52
JG 53 Pik As
JG 54 Grünherz
JG 71
JG 77 Herz As

JG 186 Trägerstaffel
JGr 200
JG 300
JG 301
JG 302
JG 400

Ergänzungsjagdgruppen

Erg.JGr. Merseburg
Erg.JGr. Süd
Erg.J.Gr. West
Erg.JGr. Ost

EJG 1
EJG 2

I. Gruppe

II. Gruppe

III. Gruppe   or   to 1941

IV. Gruppe   or

IV. Gruppe Jabo

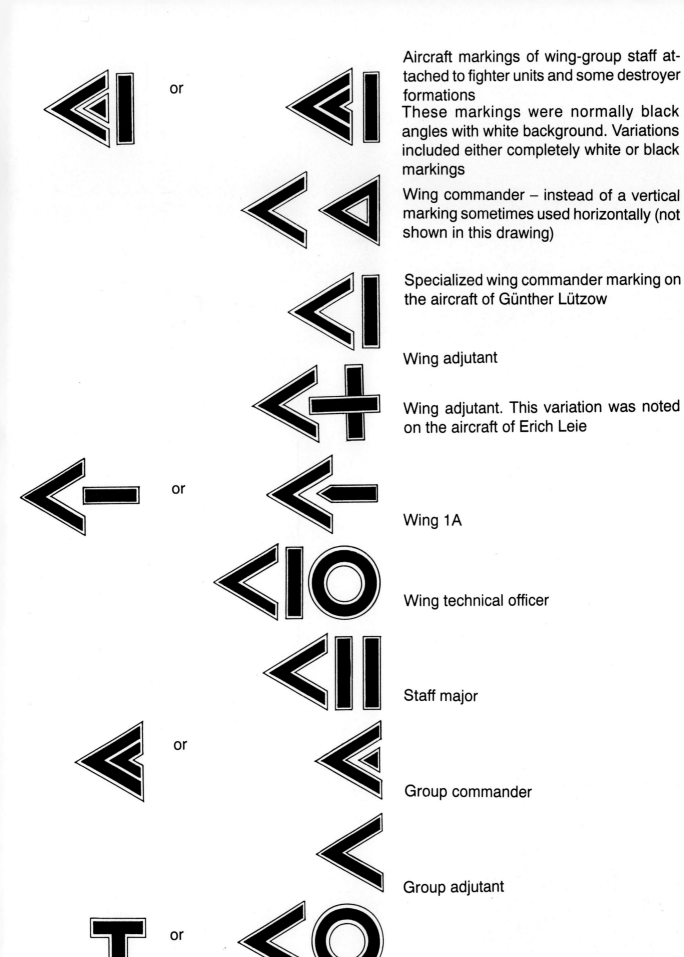

or

Aircraft markings of wing-group staff attached to fighter units and some destroyer formations
These markings were normally black angles with white background. Variations included either completely white or black markings

Wing commander – instead of a vertical marking sometimes used horizontally (not shown in this drawing)

Specialized wing commander marking on the aircraft of Günther Lützow

Wing adjutant

Wing adjutant. This variation was noted on the aircraft of Erich Leie

or

Wing 1A

Wing technical officer

Staff major

or

Group commander

Group adjutant

or

Group technical officer

On September 29, 1944 Heinkel received the order to develop and build a small-sized or "midget" turbo-fighter, which should be registered as Heinkel He 162. On December 6, 1944 it made its maiden flight! Only JG 1 was re-equipped with He 162A and made several sorties, thereby scoring two kills. Depicted is "Red 2" of 2./JG 1 around April/May 1945 on an airfield in northern Germany. Below the cabin the unit emblem is visible.

This He 162 belongs to I./JG 1. It's marked with provisional Balkenkreuze only. The photo was probably taken in April/May 1945 in Leck/Holstein.

The rudder of Haupt. "Ali" Griener's Bf 109E, WNr. 1094955. At the time of this photo, May 1942, Griener was flying with I./JG 1. He scored his first kills with 5./JG 52: a Fairey Battle on May 14, 1940, and two Spitfires on October 20 and 29, 1940. After his transfer to I./JG 1 he increased his score with two Bristol Blenheims on September 15, 1941 and May 17, 1942. He also fired some 2500 kg of ammunition during strafing missions against ground targets.

Shown here at Hopsten airfield in March/April 1944, is Maj. Emil Schnoor, Gruppenkommandeur of I./JG 1, after receiving the order to start via telephone. The phone cable leading into the Fw 190A cockpit is clearly visible. A double "M", the pilot's emblem, is painted on the fuselage just below the forward part of the cockpit. This personal emblem refers to his wife and he still displays it today on his car!

The "operator" of "angle 3", the Gruppenadjutant's plane of III./JG 1, parked the Fw 190A in a space-saving but rather unconventional manner on a farm. Also unusual is the double marking: the adjutant's angle and the figure "3." Further interesting details are the extracted flaps, the footrest, the cartridge-ejection slots for the MG 151/20 at the wingroots, as well as the exhaust pipes between the undercarriage legs.

The 1000th sortie of 7./JG 1 is credited to this Bf 109E in 1942 in Sylt, a temporary station of the Staffel. Note the Maltese cross, and the Geschwader emblem, below the canopy. The plane presumably once belonged to II. Gruppe as is indicated by the painted-over bar right of the Balkenkreuz.

The unit emblem of 7./JG 1: lightning-spitting devil within a cloud! It was seen on a Bf 109E in Sylt.

St. Pol, August 1941: Erich Leie, Geschwaderadjutant of JG 2, just returned from a successful sortie. Note the markings on this Bf 109F, probably a combination of the Geschwader and the Geschwaderadjutant's marking.

Armorers busy with MG 17s 7.9mm, of a jacked-up Bf 109E of III./JG 2 during the summer of 1940. On its fuselage the Messerschmitt bears the markings of a Major of staff (Stab) and additionally the serpentine, the emblem of III. Gruppe. Beginning in spring of 1941, the serpentine was replaced by a narrow vertical bar.

Hans "Assi" Hahn, Gruppenkommandeur of III./JG 2, with his Bf 109F probably at St. Pol in the summer of 1941. His forty-six kills are scored on the rudder. On August 14, 1941, after forty-two kills, he was awarded the Oak Leaves to the Knight's Cross. On February 21, 1943, as Gruppenkommandeur of II./JG 54 after scoring 108 kills, Hahn had to make a forced landing behind Russian lines near Demjansk after engine trouble. He was then taken prisoner.

Refueling the Bf 109F of a Major of staff in III./JG 2, probably in St. Pol in the summer of 1941. The bar at the fuselage is the new Gruppe marking. On the engine cowling is the emblem with the cock, initiated by Hans "Assi" Hahn, Gruppenkommandeur of III./JG 2. The pilot views his score-marks on the rudder.

In front of the same Bf 109F the pilot and his "Black Men" (maintenance crew). Note the cock emblem of III. Gruppe applied on both sides. The photos were probably taken in St. Pol in the summer of 1941.

The spring of 1941 at the Bernay, France airfield: Heinz Jahner of 9./JG 2 waiting for the start sign to his next sortie. JG 2 machines, like this Bf 109E, display both the Staffel emblem, and the Geschwader emblem. JG 2 was named "Richthofen Geschwader" after the famous World War I fighter ace Manfred Freiherr von Richthofen.

Roquancourt, France, fall 1941. The 9./JG 2 was nicknamed "Gnat Staffel" (Stechmückenstaffel) after its Staffel emblem. Matching the Staffel color it showed a gnat in a yellow roundel. A close view of the photo leads to the conclusion that the entire engine cowling of this Bf 109F is also painted yellow. Note the inertia starter crank below Heinz Jahner.

Even though somewhat blurred, photographs of the 2./JG 5 emblem on a Bf 109E are rare. It is shown here in the fall of 1941 in Lister, Norway.

1st/Mechanic and his protégé, a Fw 190A of 12./JG 5 in Herdla, Norway, January-February 1945. Hanging under the fuselage is a seldom used type of 300 liter drop-tank. The machine is equipped with two MG 131/13, located above the engine, and four MG 151/20 under the wings. Far right on the underside of the left wing is the bulge of the cartridge ejection slot.

Herdla, Norway, March/April 1945: Pilot Wolfgang Dietrich of 12./JG 5 had the name of his girlfriend Erika painted on his "Blue 8." Beneath this inscription the footrest can be seen, an aid for easy access to the cockpit. To the right of the Balkenkreuz is the tactical emblem of IV. Gruppe.

Herdla, Norway, March/April 1945: Three Fw 190As of 15./JG 5 are parked at the north side of the airfield, ready for their next mission. Their 300 liter drop-tanks are already mounted. It was no fun to land on Herdla's woodplanked runway when it was wet from rain, pilot's stated.

A Fw 190A with the Staffel insignia of 2./JG 11 in Husum, early summer 1943. In May 1943, the newly activated 2./JG 11 initiated a competition for a Staffel emblem. With his draft showing a pilot "misusing" Uncle Sam's top hat, Franz Steiner won the competition. By June 1943, all machines of the unit bore this emblem.

The photo of this heavy-armed "bomber killer" (Bombertöters) was probably also taken in 1943 in Husum. In addition to two MG 17 7.9mm guns over the engine, this Fw 190A is equipped with six MG 151/20s of which four were mounted in pairs in so-called weapons pods underwing. These pods came as kits to be installed by the unit mechanic when required.

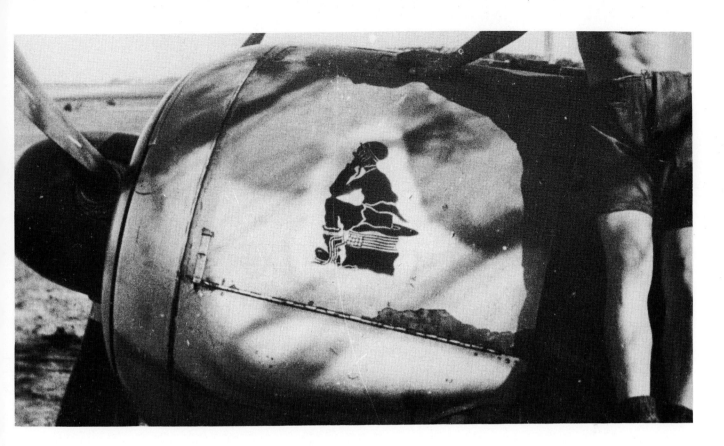

Husum, summer 1943: the "Uncle Sam" emblem on a Fw 190A of 2./JG 11.

Pilot Siegfried Rudschinat of 2./JG 11, leaving his Fw 190A, signed "Napp", in Husum – probably in late summer 1943. Rudschinat frequently used the "1", originally the Staffelkapitän's machine. "Napp" was his nickname in the squadron.

Stand-by of 3./JG 11 in Husum in the summer of 1943. For fast interception of enemy aircraft, two machines had to be ready for immediate take-off between early morning and sunset. Close to the Fw 190A "9" is the starting generator carriage to get the engine running in case of an alarm.

Husum, summer 1943: The maintenance crew, the "black men." They were responsible for getting the Fw 190As of 3./JG 11 ready for new missions.

During heavy rainfall the subsoil of airfields like that of Husum is turned to a muddy plain. To maintain and increase its serviceability the runway was covered with wood planking. The Fw 190As of 3./JG 11 are shown here waiting for whatever will come.

Since JG 20 consisted of only I. Gruppe, the Bf 109 of its Kommandeur, Hannes Trautloft, also displays the angle of the Geschwaderkommodore. On July 4, 1940 this group became III./JG 51, and kept its old emblem.

A Bf 109E displays a circle behind the Gruppenadjutant's angle, identifying it as the machine of the Gruppe TO (technical officer). Werner Pichon Kalau von Hofe, TO of I./JG 20 initiated this marking for all fighter units. Photo taken in fall 1939.

Covered with camouflage nets, this JG 26 Bf 109E is serviced by a mechanic. Easily recognizable is the crank, used to turn the inertia starter before the magneto is energized and the engine engaged. The high-drawn light blue on the fuselage and the two-green segments on wings and upper fuselage indicate this time period as 1940.

At the armory Düsseldorf in spring 1940, an armorer works on the two MG 17 7.9mm guns located above the engine and firing through the airscrew-disk area. This Bf 109E of 6./JG 26 is jacked-up to adjust the weapons. On the fuselage the machine still displays the white outlined narrow 1939 style Balkenkreuz.

An unusual version of the 7./JG 26 emblem is displayed on this Bf 109E. Normally the red heart of 7. Staffel was applied without blazon. Here, too, the date of the picture can be appointed by the camouflage scheme of the aircraft as spring 1940.

June 1944 at Gyancourt near Versailles, France near the invasion front. At this time camouflage was essential to stay alive. Even changing the engine as done on this Fw 190A of 7./JG 26 needed to be made in the "undergrowths" only to avoid attracting the attention of the ubiquitous gentlemen on the other side. About twenty-two score marks can be noted at the rudder of the presumably "Yellow 3." It is probably the machine of Staffelkapitän Waldemar Radener. He was awarded the Knight's Cross on March 12, 1945 and at the end of the war his final score stood at thirty-six kills, sixteen of them four-engine bombers.

A Schwarm of 7./JG 26 aircraft. The time period of this photo must be around April/May 1944 before the D-Day invasion. Twenty score marks can be made out on the rudder of number "4." This may also be one of Waldemar Radener's aircraft.

ATTENTION! CANOPY DROPPED BY EXPLOSIVE! This sign was part of the head armor plate of the Fw 190D, shown here during the summer of 1944 at airfield E 21 Klausheide near Nordhorn. Shown is Lt. "Pitt" Andel of 7./JG 26 fastening his seat belts assisted by a member of his ground crew.

In December 1944, II./JG 26 was re-equipped to the new Fw 190D in Reinsehlen. With this type the day-fighters were given a machine equal to those of Allied fighter units. In contrary to the A-version, it had an in-line rather than radial engine. The opened radiator flaps are clearly visible. To have the tactical number, here the "9", applied on the rudder, is rather unusual.

This photo was also taken in December 1944 in Reinsehlen during re-equipping of II./JG 26 to Fw 190Ds. This machine has a different camouflage scheme and displays the normal Balkenkreuz, contrary to the photo above. Here the radiator flaps are closed.

This photo was taken at a dusty airfield somewhere in North Africa and shows a Bf 109E belonging to the Gruppenadjutant of I./JG 27. Besides the sandbrown camouflage the machine bears a white fuselage band, indicating the Mediterranean theater of operations.

The Bf 109E-trop of the Staffelkapitän of I./JG 27 Karl-Wolfgang Redlich in spring/summer 1941. The rudder of the machine already displays fifteen score marks. After twenty-one victories Redlich was awarded the Knight's Cross on July 9, 1941. He increased this number in air-combat against four-engine bombers to forty-three until May 29, 1944 when he, then Kommandeur of I./JG 27, was killed in action.

JG 27 in Africa. "White 1" a Bf 109F-trop could have been the aircraft of a Staffelkapitän. Typical for the North African theater are the white-colored wing tips, the fuselage band and the front part of the engine.

A communication and courier aircraft of I./JG 27 in Innsbruck in 1941. This Bf 108B with the code TI+EX still displays the standard camouflage: upper surfaces with green segments, and underside light blue. Note the open freight hatch and the landing light under the left wing.

Many questions about these photos are still unanswered! "White 5" is a Me 262A, WNr. 111745, and probably belongs to JV 44. It can also be assumed that the photos were shot in München-Riem in spring 1945.

At the Stabstaffel of JG 51 "Mölders" it was customary for a while to "baptize" the individual aircraft. Fritz "Paule" Lüddecke baptized his Fw 190A "Black 6" Hanni. Lüddecke was awarded the Knight's Cross posthumously on November 18, 1944. Before, on August 10, 1944 during one of his many strafing raids near Wilkowischken, East Prussia, and after his fiftieth victory, he was shot down by Russian flak and killed.

Lt. Heym also had his Fw 190A "baptized." In fall 1944 his "Black 11" was embellished with the name "Tanja", the pilot's second love.

This photo taken at Speyer in 1939 shows aircraft of I./JG 51. In the foreground is the Bf 109E of Gruppenadjutant Joseph Priller. Beneath the cockpit is his personal emblem, the Ace of Hearts (Herz-As) with the name "Jutta." "Pips" scored 101 kills in the West and was awarded the Swords to the Knight's Cross.

Geschwader-Ia. Lt. Terry, displays his personal emblem, a terrier on his Bf 109E. In the fall of 1939, JG 51 consisted of I. Gruppe only. With a mountain goat as group emblem, his machine already bears the markings of the Geschwader-Ia. The Geschwaderstab was established later, at the end of 1939.

Spring 1940 in Krefeld-Uerdingen. Again Lt. Terry's Bf 109E with the "Aiblinger Gams" emblem of I./JG 51. Also of interest are the numbers along the fuselage, numbering the bulkheads of the frame.

To the right of the I./JG 51 emblem is another emblem which resembles a "Royal Lion." Its meaning is unknown. To the right of the adjutant's angle the yellow octane triangle is seen, which indicates this aircraft's DB 601 engine requires 87 octane fuel.

Replacing DB 601 Aa engine on a Bf 109E of I./JG 51 in Krefeld-Uerdingen in 1940. Visible are the two offset mounted MG 17 7.9mm guns over the engine.

Ready for take-off! Last minute touches for the Bf 109E of JG 51 Geschwader-Ia., Lt. Terry, in the summer of 1940. On this machine's light blue fuselage sides the red and gray dots are already sprayed on.

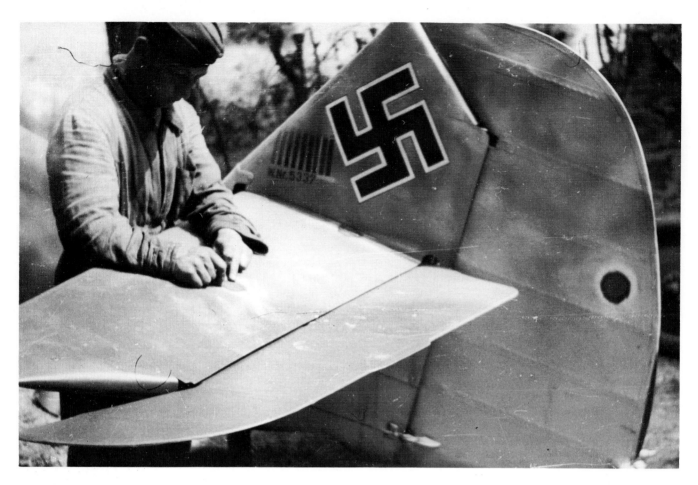

Saddler Karl Schild of I./JG 51 maintenance crew at work. Damage by enemy rounds must be repaired. Nine kill marks on the rudder of this I./JG 51 Bf 109E, WNr. 5337, are visible.

Damage on the same aircraft, "White 3" of Uffz. Schmidt a pilot with I./JG 51. After his tenth kill over London he was listed as missing in action.

Shown here is the Bf 109F "Red 1" of squadron leader Heinz Schuman 2./JG 51. The Geschwader emblem as well as the Staffel emblem are displayed. Schuman was awarded the Knight's Cross on March 18, 1943 after his eighteenth victory. He was killed in action on November 8, 1943 near Charleroi fighting Spitfires as Kommodore of SKG 10.

Another photo of Heinz Schuman's "Red 1." An ETC 50/VIII d for four 50 kg. bombs is fitted under the fuselage. Pipes are mounted to the fins of the bombs to produce a howling sound while falling.

Sub-zero temperatures and the lack of hangars on Russian airfields led to many improvised but useful ideas for maintaining aircraft. Forty-seven kill marks are painted on the rudder of this Bf 109F "Red 7" of 3./JG 51. This plane was flown by Heinrich "Gaudi" Krafft, who was awarded the Knight's Cross on March 18, 1942. This photo was taken in Stolzy, in January/February 1942.

The aircraft of Josef "Joschko" Fözö, Kommandeur of II./JG 51 in spring of 1941. Fifteen score marks are visible on the rudder of this Bf 109E, WNr. 703. The first victory is noted by an exclamation point! According to witnesses, Fözö's first kill, a French captive balloon, was also the very first victory of II./JG 51. After his twenty-second kill and with the rank of Hauptmann he was awarded the Knight's Cross on July 2, 1942.

Test running a Bf 109E of II./JG 51. As with I./JG 51, the confusing combination of unit markings as seen: angle plus vertical bar. Such markings denotes that the machine is that of the Gruppenadjutant, though the emblem of II. Gruppe is applied aft of the Balkenkreuz. Until 1939 there was no Geschwaderstab with JG 51. This perhaps explains why the machines of the Gruppenstab displayed the markings of the Geschwaderstab. Also unclear is the three ring emblem beneath the cockpit.

The shape of the "White "4" on this 4./JG 51 Bf 109E in 1940 is unusual. Painted on the rudder are the score marks for the pilot's seven kills. Applied beneath the cockpit is the personal emblem of the pilot, "Gretl 2." Sitting in the cockpit is Rolf Helber, who's fate is unknown.

Wilhelm Mink, holder of the Knight's Cross, sitting on the wing of a Bf 109G/R6-trop "White 12" of 5./JG 51 in Neubiberg. The photo was taken in fall of 1943 after the unit was transferred back to Germany from Italy. The R6 kit consisted of two each MG 151/20s in weapons pods that were fixed underwing (right). On March 12, 1945 Mink, flying his Bf 109G-14 with I./EJG 1, was killed in action near Hardersleben, Denmark during a dogfight with British fighters.

Lt. H. Seegatz of 5./JG 51 leaving the cockpit of his Bf 109E. The dubious Pomasda emblem of this machine has been shown in numerous aviation publications. Though its origin is unknown, we know he retained it through all of his units, 5./JG 51, JG 25, JG 5 and finally JG 1 before being killed in action on March 20, 1944, after thirty-one kills.

This Bf 109E "Red 6" of 5./JG 51 displays an extraordinary sign on both sides of the fuselage: "Attention, Beginner!" Members of his Staffel stated that Lt. H. Seegatz may have flown this aircraft.

Score of success on the rudder of a Bf 109F, WNr. 8120, photographed on May 16, 1942. Otto Tange previously scored three victories in the West and forty-eight in the East while with 5./JG 51. On March 19, 1942 as ranking Oberfeldwebel and with forty-one kills, he was awarded the Knight's Cross. On July 30, 1943 after sixty-eight kills he was hit by flak and crashed burning into a Russian village.

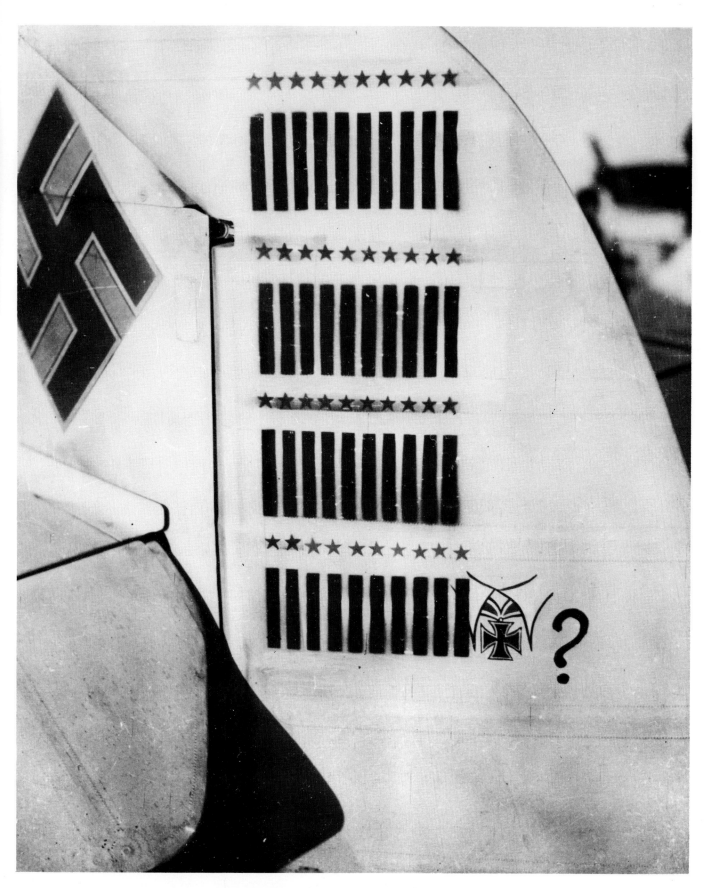

When at last will the Knight's Cross be awarded? This pilot can hardly wait after his fortieth victory in the winter of 1941/42 in Brijansk. This is a Bf 109F of 5./JG 51, presumably the machine of Hans Strelow who, at twenty years of age, was the youngest holder of the Oak Leaves to the Knight's Cross. The latter was awarded to him on March 18, 1942 after fifty-two kills, and on March 24, 1942 already with sixty-six kills he received the Oak Leaves. On May 22, 1942, after his sixty-eighth kill, a Pe-2, he made a forced landing near Novosil behind Russian lines. Preferring not to become a prisoner of war, he shot himself.

A Bf 109E "Yellow 6" of 6./JG 51 rests peacefully on German soil near Böblingen in the winter 1939/40. Herz-As (Ace of Hearts) was the Staffel emblem while Josef Priller was Staffelkapitän. When he left the unit he retained it as his personal emblem.

Uffz. Haase chose a very personal emblem. The hare with binoculars is displayed on his Bf 109E "Yellow 3" of 6./JG 51.

Unusually placed is the II. Gruppe bar on this Bf 109F, reaching into the zero of the "Yellow 10." The pilot of this machine had already scored eight kills by the end of July 1941 in Stara Bychow.

In July 1941 at Stara Bychow is Oblt. Walter and his Bf 109F "Yellow 11." At this time he was with II./JG 51. Through the open cabin-glazing the armor plate behind the headrest is visible. Many pilots owed their lives to this feature.

The pilot of this III./JG 51 Bf 109F with twenty-nine kill marks could not be identified.

The Staffelkapitän of 9./JG 51, Karl-Heinz "Bubi" Schnell stands next to the rudder of his Bf 109F which displays some thirty-eight kill markings. Schnell was awarded the Knight's Cross on August 1, 1941 after twenty-nine kills. By the end of the war, he had increased this score to seventy-two.

Sitting in his Bf 109F named "Mädi" is Edmund Wagner, Staffelkapitän of 9./JG 51. Up to his early death on November 13, 1941 near Pafmutowka, Russia, Wagner was the most successful pilot of JG 51.

This photo shows the score on the rudder of Edmund Wagner's Bf 109F. Shown are fifty-five kills, including one in the West. This photo must have been taken shortly before his death, as he was killed during a dogfight after his fifty-seventh victory. Five days later on November 17, 1941 Wagner was posthumously awarded the Knight's Cross.

This rudder is crammed with 102 kill markings. This successful score belongs to Franz Josef Beerenbrook of JG 51, who on August 3, 1942 was awarded the Oak Leaves to the Knight's Cross after his 102nd kill. However, his luck run out on November 9, 1942, though he scored three more kills, a hit into his radiator forced him to land near Welish, Russia behind Russian lines and was taken prisoner. On this day he scored kill numbers 115 through 117.

Franz Josef Beerenbrook climbing out of his Bf 109F which is the machine of the JG 51 Geschwaderadjutant. Displayed beneath the cockpit is the slightly altered "Hunter" emblem. Forward of the cockpit a bullet-proof glassplate is mounted against direct his from front.

This Bf 108B, coded DB+KY, was used for courier missions by IV./JG 51. An unusual emblem is seen on the fuselage (below). Pilot "Rübezahl" W. Zeugner waits for his "Fireman" (copilot) H. Löfflet to come aboard.

Another unorthodox landing. This time it was a pilot of II./JG 51 with his Bf 109F "9." Here the less usual emblem of a IV. Gruppe is seen, a cross instead of the circle.

One of the most famous aces of the Luftwaffe was Heinz Bär. Here we see the rudder of his Bf 109F with 113 kill marks when he was Kommandeur of IV./JG 51, during late June/early July 1942. We assume that this photo was not taken in Russia, but after he was transferred to become the Kommandeur of I./JG 77. Besides his kill marks the rudder also displays the pilot's decorations: the Knight's Cross with Oak Leaves and Swords. Bär was the seventh member of the Wehrmacht awarded the Swords after his ninetieth kill. Until the end of the war, making over 1000 sorties, he would increase his score to 220 kills, including sixteen with the Me 262.

Bf 109E, probably of III./JG 52, on an escort mission on April 21, 1941. This photo shows the machine of the Gruppenadjutant, and displays a small "1" besides the angle on the fuselage. Beneath the cockpit is the Geschwader emblem, a winged sword. The engine cowling, the wing tips, rudder and a narrow fuselage band are all yellow. Also visible, though overpainted, are four letters on the fuselage, which is the factory code.

September 1940 at the channel front. This Bf 109E bears the "Wilde Sau" (Wild Boar) emblem of I./JG 52. Behind it is the square-shaped intake scoop of the engine supercharger. Interesting are the shutters at the opening and the exhaust dampers.

This Bf 109E, "White 1," of Ergänzungsgeschwader 52 is shown on a transfer flight to Borkum, probably in December 1941. The function of the bulge at the underside of the fuselage is not entirely clear. A pilot of JG 1 has stated that it is a seldom used aerial for the FuG 16z. This was a combination radio-set/radio direction finder. It enabled radio, ground-air/air-ground communications, as well as a radio-guided approach to the receiving VHF transmitter.

In march 1944, a Bf 109G of 3./JG 53 is shown parked under makeshift camouflage at the Maniago, Italy airfield. Fitted at the fuselage centerline is a 300 liter droptank, and fixed aft of the cockpit is the loop aerial for the radio-set FuG 16. Dark spots on the rudder seem to be patched bullet hits.

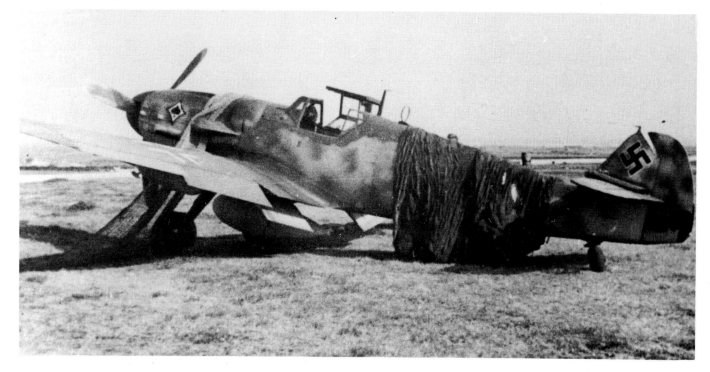

Sciacca, Sicily in June 1943. Walter Reinicke climbing out of his Bf 109G "White 9" of 7./JG 53. The personal emblem painted on the fuselage is quite ingenious, though its origin is still unclear. Reinicke took over this aircraft from a pilot of his Staffel who was killed in action in another aircraft. Also on the aircraft is the emblem of JG 53, "Pik As," and beneath it the inscription "Seemann" (sailor).

A thankless task for a fighter pilot was flying escort. With slightly extracted flaps this Bf 109F of 7./JG 53 remains within the speed range of its charge over the Mediterranean in 1942. The white fuselage band denotes the Mediterranean theater of operations, and probably also to the southern section of the Eastern front.

Christmas party at III./JG 53 in Wiesbaden, 1939. All of these Bf 109Es belong to 7./JG 53. Of interest is the varying style of the white number on the fuselages. Some are black outlined, some not. Aft of the Balkenkreuz the vertical bar for III. Gruppe is placed.

Not much is known about this photo of a 10./JG 53 Bf 109F, part of a Jabo-Gruppe. It was probably taken in 1942 or 1943 in Sicily. The emblem of the IV. Jabo-Gruppe, a falling bomb, is painted to the left of the white fuselage band.

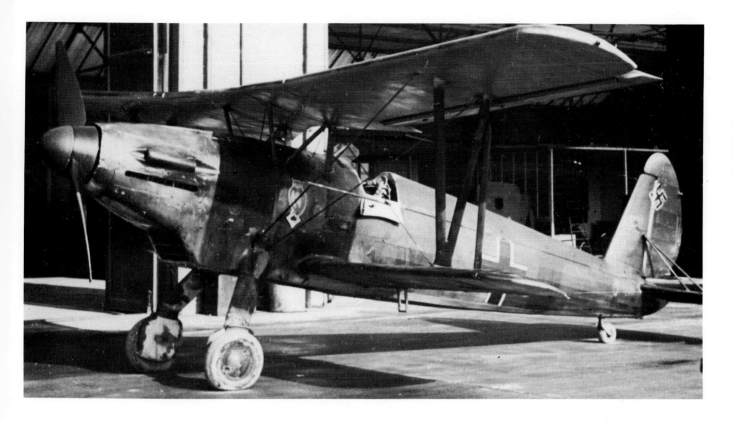

Shown here is an Arado Ar 68E in Mannheim, 1939. At 10.(N)/JG 53 it was flying improvised nightfighter missions. Still displaying its original finish, the main wheel fairings had been removed.

From the early missions to England to the Eastern front, Hannes Trautloft led his JG 54 as Kommodore for three years. At least twenty-one kill marks can be recognized on the rudder of his Bf 109F later summer 1941. Shortly before, on July 27, 1941, he was awarded the Knight's Cross after twenty kills. Until July 1943 he increased his score to fifty-seven victories. Trautloft then left the Geschwader to work as Inspector East in the staff of the General of Fighter Forces. Note the yellow engine cowling and propeller tips of Trautloft's machine.

On this Fw 190A of Geschwaderstab JG 54 the emblems of all three Gruppen can be seen next to the Geschwader emblem: top left the city emblem of Nürnberg for I. Gruppe, at right the emblem of Wien-Aspern for II. Gruppe and, below, the Jesau-cross with three aircraft silhouettes for III. Gruppe. This photo was probably taken in the winter of 1942/43 in Russia after re-equipping from Bf 109s to Fw 190As. This Fw 190A perhaps belonged to another unit. On the engine cowling and forward of the Balkenkreuz is an emblem respectively a number was overpainted. Except for the yellow fuselage band, the entire upper surfaces of the machine are painted white as winter camouflage.

This Bf 109E with its intense camouflage was already flown in summer, 1940, by Hubertus von Bonin, Kommandeur of I./JG 54. The Gruppenkommandeur angle is here in white, a style that appeared randomly from 1944 to the end of the war. The "Mickey Mouse" insignia was carried over from the Spanish civil war, where von Bonin had scored four air victories. Von Bonin was awarded the Knight's Cross on December 21, 1942, after fifty-one kills. After his seventy-seventh victory he was shot down during air combat near Witebsk, Russia on December 15, 1943.

A chimney sweep is supposed to bring luck! What is not known is whether this happened to the pilot of this Bf 109E "White 8" with its intense camouflage. This chimney sweep is a variant of the emblem of I./JG 54 "Grunherz." Staffel emblems often appeared in many versions.

This intensely camouflaged Bf 109E also belongs to I./JG 54, and it displays a more frequently used variant of the chimney sweep Staffel emblem. The paint of "White 9" has partially flaked off.

Summer 1941 at Mal-Owitsch, Russia. A mechanic checks the engine of a Bf 109F of the 1./JG 54 Staffelkapitän Reinhard Seiler. By this time Seiler had scored his first eighteen kills. After forty-two victories, Seiler was awarded the Knight's Cross on December 20, 1941, and the Oak Leaves after his 100th on March 2, 1944. At this period he was already seriously wounded and for the rest of the war physically unfit for duty as combat pilot. The machine in the background belongs to the Kommandeur of I./JG 54.

White winter camouflage is displayed on this fighter-bomber (Jabo) of I./JG 54 in the winter 1941/42, presumably in Gatschina, Russia. On the fuselage-ETC of this Bf 109F is a 250 kg bomb. The mainwheel fairings are removed for easier taxiing on the snow-covered airfield.

This devil insignia belonged to 2./JG 54 – at least as a Staffel emblem on this particular Bf 109E in 1940. To the left of the emblem is the nameplate and just above it the lubrication triangle with the inscription "Redring."

"Hamänchen" was the personal signature of fighter pilot Peter Bremer of 2./JG 54. His Bf 109F "Red 12" is already marked with eight kill markings on the rudder.

In this emblem the "Wild Huntsman" of 3./JG 54 shot down two Spitfires with his blunderbuss. Normally this insignia was framed by a shield, however on this Bf 109E "Yellow 5" the shield was left off when it was flying its missions in 1940.

This Bf 109 E of I./JG 77 is shown here on the airfield of Gleiwitz. In November 1941 this unit was renamed IV./JG 51. The Gruppe emblem, the tattered boot, is seen on the engine cowling. The propeller blades bear the letters VDM in a white triangle –the abbreviation of "Vereinigte Deutsche Metallwerke."

The tail of "Red 10" lifts off the ground. Aft of the fuselage Balkenkreuz is the top-hat emblem of I./JG 77. This Bf 109, just taking off in St. Omer, France in 1941, however belongs to IV./JG 51, the former I./JG 77. Note the all yellow nose of the machine.

Lt. "Bubi" Kuntze, Gruppenadjutant of I./JG 77, painted a "rascal" on his Bf 109E as a reference to his nickname. In fall of 1940, Lt. Kuntze was killed in action over the Channel front.

A personal emblem similar to Lt. Kuntze's is displayed here on Heinz Klöpper's Bf 109E. It can be assumed that both emblems were created by the very same artist. Klöpper was shot down on May 21, 1940 near Dinant at the Maas river. To defend himself he kept his pistol drawn while descending in his parachute. This event is depicted in his emblem.

In the summer of 1940 this Bf 109E of I./JG 77 struck the ground like the lightning bolt emblazoned on its fuselage. This decorative painting on "Black 13" is outstanding and therefore it can be concluded that it stems from Lt. "Gockel" Hahn's creativity. As a pilot with I./JG 77 he was also the Gruppe's artist and created many personal emblems.

Heinrich Seeling with his chief mechanic in Harge, Ostfriesland in October 1939. Seelinger was Staffelkapitän of 6./JG 186(T) the Luftwaffe's carrier squadron. Interesting is the Staffel emblem: the coat of arms of Graf Zeppelin, the famous creator of airships. The only German aircraft carrier was named after him and bore this emblem at her bow. 6./JG 186(T) was designated as a carrier-based fighter unit (the (T) stands for "Träger = Carrier). However, the vessel was never completed and was sunk in the Baltic Sea after the Russians attempted to tow her away.

This Bf 109E is the machine of Haupt. Tobitsch, Staffelkapitän of 6./JG 186(T). He was shot down on May 10, 1940 in the area of Der Helder/de Kooy, Holland, made a belly-landing and was taken prisoner by Dutch troops. The members of his Staffel nicknamed him "The Old Man," and it is this nickname that appears on his machine beneath the cockpit. Unusual is the fuselage band, which is the marking for III. Gruppe, though the machine belongs to II. Gruppe. Stationed around 1940 in Norway, II./JG 186(T) was renamed III./JG 77. At this time the aircraft carrier project was canceled, and thus was also the end for carrier-based fighter units.

Eberhard Gzik and his Bf 109G "Rita" of 2./JG 300 in Borkheide around October/November 1944. The person at his left cannot be identified. Remarkable is the new Erla full-vision canopy, common with the G-versions of the Bf 109. The broad black fuselage band is the marking for all Geschwadern belonging to Reich Defense units. Many fighter units in the West bore such fuselage bands.

This photo of a Bf 109K "17" of 2./JG 300 was also taken in Borkheide around October/November 1944. Sitting in the cockpit is Lt. "Jupp" Jordan, Eberhard Gzik's Rottenflieger (wingman). Note that the head armor behind the pilot is fastened to the Erla-canopy so that they both swing aside when opened.

Einsatzkommando Orange, with the strength of a Staffel and commanded by Heinz Bär in Marignac, Marseille around 1943-1944. Pilot Siegfried Sy presenting himself with his "1" Bf 109 G/R6 (R6 = field kit 6, consisting of two weapons pods with two MG 151/ 20mm fixed underwing). Note the radiator, extracted flaps, weapon hole in the spinner closed with a plug, and the scribbled propeller blade. Further the bulge beneath the starter crank.

II./JG 132 "Richthofen" in 1936 in Jüterbog near Berlin. Every Geschwader had its own identification color; for JG 132 it was red. The white circle on the He 51C "8" indicates that this machine belongs to the third Staffel of a Gruppe, in this case 6. Staffel. After the "8" should be a horizontal bar, the marking for II. Gruppe, as can be seen a on number "1." Angle – triangle – bar means Gruppenstab II. Gruppe, aircraft of the flight leader (Kettenführer). Later on this was the marking for the Gruppenkommandeur of II. Gruppe.

This He 51 C of 6./JG 132 produced its nose-over in Jüterbog in 1936. As can be seen, the markings were worn at all four sides. The number "1" under the drop-tank indicates this machine as the first within 6. squadron.

A pilot and his mechanics with an He 51A, taken in 1938 in Schweinfurt. Unfortunately we do not know to which fighter Geschwader this machine belonged. So much is revealed by the markings: it belongs to 2. Staffel of I. Gruppe. The fuselage rings forward and aft always mark 2. Staffel of a Gruppe. The lack of markings for II. or III. Gruppe clearly indicates this He 51 belongs to I. Gruppe.

Aircraft with unusual markings appear once in a while, such as this Fw 190A with the yellow fuselage code "zero", Balkenkreuz and Gruppe bar for III. Gruppe. The period and location of this photo are also unclear, as is the Geschwader it belongs to.

Bad luck for test pilot Ernst Büchner of AGO aircraft factory in Oschersleben with his brand new Fw 190A, WNr. 9244, on December 10, 1944. After only one minute of flying time he had engine trouble and crash-landed the machine on a field near Oschersleben – right into a hunting party! The hunters must have been shocked when they saw the pilot clad in women's clothing climbing out of the aircraft! Someone had bet ten cigarettes that Büchner would not dare to fly in such a disguise. Notable is the dome-shaped canopy, first used on the Fw 190F and later also on the A-version.

The bitter end of the glorious Luftwaffe after surrender on May 8, 1945 in Flensburg. Numerous Fw 190A and D without propellers waiting to be scrapped.

157

CHAPTER V

Zerstörer and Night Fighter Units of the Luftwaffe

Zerstörerverbände
ZG 1 zweimal aufgestellt
I.+V. (Z)/LG 1
ZG 2 zweimal aufgestellt
ZG 26 zweimal aufgestellt
ZG 51
Zg 52
Zg 76 zweimal aufgestellt
ZG 101

Erprobungsgruppe 210
V./KG 40

Nachtjagdverbände
NJG 1
NJG 2
NJG 3
NJG 4
NJG 5
NJG 6
NJG 7
NJGr 10
NJG 11
NJG 100
NJG 101
NJG 102
NJG 200

NJ-Staffel Finnland/Norwegen
NJ-Schwarm Luftflotte 1
NJ-Schwarm Luftflotte 4
NJ-Schwarm Luftflotte 6
NJ-Schwarm Luftkdo.Don
NJ-Schwarm Luftkdo.Ost

JG 300
JG 301
JG 302
V./KG 2

Luftbeobachterstaffel 1-7

Behelfsbeleuchterstaffel 1 & 2
III.(Beleuchter)/KG 3

Versuchskdo. E-Stelle Werneuchen
10.(N)/ZG 26
10.(N)/ZG 53

As shown here in Dortmund during the summer of 1939, the arched tomcat was the emblem of IV.(L)/JG 134. Later on and somewhat re-styled, 8./ZG 26 adopted it. To the right is the yellow triangle with the inscription "87 octane" and just above it a further one with "Aero Shell medium."
page 159

A large wasp was the nose art on both sides of a Zerstörergeschwader 1 Bf 110. This photo shows an engine test-run on a Bf 110 of 4./ZG 1 at Sestschinskaja, Russia in September 1941.

This photo of a Me 210 was taken in the Mediterranean area, presumably at Sicily towards the end of 1942. At this time Sicily was the operational area of III./ZG 1. Note the openings in the nose for the MG-muzzles.

The "Black Men" (maintenance crew), keep this Me 210 of III./ZG 1 ready for operations in November/December 1942 at Trapani, Sicily. On the upper side of the DB 601 F engine just above the supercharger inlet are two window-like openings. Behind them facing towards the fuselage were engine control instruments. The reason for two opposite windows on each engine is its interchangeability: whether the engine was mounted on port or starboard, only the instruments had to be adjusted to face toward the fuselage.

At Trapani, Sicily, March 1943, this Me 210A of III./ZG 1 waits for its next mission. On the fuselage nose are openings for the muzzles of two MG 17 7.9mm and two MG 151/20mm.

For a short period in spring/summer 1939, 3./ZG 76 displayed the city emblem of Olmütz as its Staffel emblem. These photos of a Bf 110B were possibly taken at Olmütz in April 1939.

Summer 1940. Shown here crossing the snow-covered hills of Norway is a very rare Bf 110D of I./ZG 76, still displaying the old code SE+ZT. To increase the operating range the Bf 110D, a 1200-liter belly-tank was added, unventilated and as an integrated part of the fuselage. The D-version therefore was nicknamed "Dackelbauch" (Dachschund-belly).

Though the emblem of 3./ZG 76 is poorly depicted in this photo, it is shown for two reasons: 1) it is one of the very few to show this emblem on an aircraft, and 2) its assignment has to be corrected: Aviation literature erroneously assigns this emblem often to 5./ZG 76. This photo shows Ofw. Fleischmann in his Bf 110C in Westerland, Sylt in April 1940, shortly before the Norwegian campaign.

The parking area of 5./ZG 76 in Böblingen in April 1940. The Bf 110Cs with the "sharkmouth" are those of II. Gruppe. In the background is M8+FN.

The nose of the Bf 110C is an ideal canvas for the "shark mouth." II./ZG 76 displayed this war paint since spring 1940. This photo was probably taken in the winter of 1940/41 at the Swinemünde airfield Garz/Usedom.

As in the photo at the bottom of page 163, this one shows a Bf 110C of II./ZG 76 at the Swinemünde airfield Garz, Usedom in the winter of 1940/41.

As a very effective defense armament, some Bf 110Es were equipped with two backward firing MG 17/7.9mm guns on both sides of the fuselage. For precise aiming the rear-view sight scope RF 1 A was mounted. This photo was taken in 1942 in the North African theater of operations. This Bf 110E presumably belongs to a reconnaissance unit rather than a Zerstörer formation.

This Bf 110C parked in April/May 1940 under camouflage nets at Krefeld/Uerdingen displays the emblem of Westphalia. It could not be clear as to which Zerstörer unit this emblem was assigned.

This Bf 110C is brand new. The machine is neatly painted two-green (70/71) and light-blue (65). The photo was taken in winter 1939/1940 in Mannheim. Note that the hangar doors are already camouflaged.

Pilot Hans Raab and his Bf 110 of ZG 1 pose for the photographer. Two different Geschwader emblems are painted on the fuselage: to the left is the ZG 1 wasp, and under the glazing the emblem of I./SKG 210. Nevertheless, this aircraft definitely belongs to ZG 1. Many crews of the late SKG 210 changed to ZG 1.

This photo of a rudder is difficult to explain. As can be seen, the fourth of the marked fourteen victories is for an aircraft in the Swiss Air Force. In June 1940, II./ZG 1 was renamed JG 101 and had frequent hostile contact with Swiss fighters. After the French campaign the unit became III./ZG 76, and on April 24, 1941 it was renamed again to II./SKG 210. According to the owner of the photo, a former member of I./SKG 210, it taken in late summer 1941 at Sestschinskaja, Russia. Wolfgang Schenk (Knight's Cross on August 14, 1941, Oak Leaves on October 30, 1942), at this time Staffelkapitän of 1./SKG 210, could have been the pilot of this machine.

This engine run-up test on a Bf 110 of II./SKG 210 was photographed in October 1941 at the airfield of Chaikowka. Note the code S9+?? of SKG 210 (sometimes also ZG 1 with 2N+??) and the wasp nose of ZG 1.

Improvised night fighting missions, though with little success, were flown with this Arado Ar 68E in winter 1939 from the Böblingen airfield. The night-black machine is coded N+21.

Parked presumably at the NJG 1 airfield Lister, Norway in February 1942 was this Bf 108. Used for courier missions, the aircraft displays the night fighter emblem on the fuselage.

Also taken at Lister, Norway in February 1942 was this picture of a Bf 110 of NJG 1. Clearly visible is the "England Lightning" emblem used by all night fighter units. This Geschwader emblem originated from the family coat of arms of Wolfgang Falck, NJG 1, one of the originators of the night fighter arm.

Formation flight of 7./NJG 1 aircraft over the Baltic Sea towards the end of 1941. Shown is Bf 110 with code G9+DR and the night fighter camouflage: black all over. The emblem on the fuselage is hardly visible. At the time this photo was shot, night fighter missions were flown without radar equipment.

A Ju 88 C of 3./NJG 2. As can be seen, the exhaust pipes are covered with flame dampers to decrease the danger of being spotted by enemy aircraft.

Participants in Operation "Donnerkeil" (Thunderbolt) – the Channel breakthrough of the German battle ships Scharnhorst, Gneisenau, and Admiral Hipper between February 11-13, 1942 as part of their transfer from Brest to Wilhelmshafen resp. Kiel – this motley bunch of night fighter aircraft temporarily remained at Lister, Norway. These photos were taken on February 25, 1942. G9+MT of 9./NJG 1, G9+DU of 10./NJG 1 and D5+KS of 8./NJG 3 can be recognized. II./ZG 76 became III./NJG 3 and kept its old "sharkmouth" emblem for quite a while.

A Bf 110G night fighter equipped with FuG 212 radar set at the airfield Greifswald-Kollberg. The C9+BT belongs to 9./NJG 5. Other interesting details are the "England Lightning" emblem, the 300-liter underwing drop-tanks and the monstrous exhaust flame dampers.

According to its code C9+AD, this Bf 110G parked at Königsberg should be the machine of the Kommandeur of III./NJG 5. The "D" stands for Stab III./NJG 5. Visible in the background a He 177 and a Ju 88 with rather large numbers at the rudder. These aircraft were probably not operational.

Major Leuchs at his obituary speech during the funeral ceremony for Maj. Heinrich Wohlers, Kommandeur I./NJG 6, holder of the Knight's Cross (awarded to him on January 1, 1944). Wohlers was killed on March 15, 1944 when he crash-landed at the fogged-in airfield at Stuttgart-Echterdingen. Behind Leuchs a Bf 110G of I./NJG 6 with FuG 212 radar set.

Bf 110G of 2./NJG 6 returning in formation from "Blindworm" (code for transferring from a dispersal landing field to an airfield with night-landing and take-off facilities), towards the end of 1944. Note the large funnel-shaped flame dampers of the MK 108/30mm cannons between the aerials of FuG 220 "Liechtenstein" radar set. Also the further the bulky tubes of the exhaust flame dampers and the 300-liter underwing drop-tanks. In the foreground flies 2Z+GK.

There were also night fighter versions of the Do 217, such as the J-series. Despite its very long range and heavy armament, it was too slow for night fighting missions. These aircraft were flown primarily on the Eastern front and at night fighter training units. Beneath the cockpit is the "England-Lightning" emblem. Unit unknown.

This destroyer-type Bf 110G-2/R1 waits at Böblingen for its next defense mission. With the 37mm cannon under the fuselage, a derivative of the anti-aircraft gun Flak 18, the aircraft was well armed. During flight the weapon could be reloaded from the cockpit where twelve clips with six rounds each were stored. A direct hit on a four-engine bomber had a devastating effect. However, this armament made the machine very clumsy and easy prey to Allied escort fighters.

Chapter VI

Bomber Units of the Luftwaffe

Following is a list of the most important bomber groups

Lehrgeschwader LG 1
Lehrgeschwader LG 2

KG 1 Hindenburg
KG 2 Holzhammer
KG 3 Blitzgeschwader
KG 4 General Wever
KG 6
KG 26 Löwengeschwader
KG 27 Boelke
KG 28
KG 30 Adlergeschwader
KG 40
FKG 50

KG 51 Edelweiss
KG 53 Legion Condor
KG 54 Totenkopf
KG 55
KG 60
KG 66
KG 76
KG 77
KG 100 Wiking
KG 200
KGr. 606
KGr 806
KG 101 (vorher Kampfschulgeschwader KSG

Markings of combat aircraft

In 1939 a new system for aircraft markings was initiated. The number/letter combination ahead of the fuselage Balkenkreuz identified the unit to which the aircraft belonged. The first letter after the Balkenkreuz identified the aircraft alphabetically within a Staffel and was often printed in Staffel colors. The last letter indicated the Stab/Staffel and simultaneously the Gruppe.

1. Beispiel: He 111 A1+AA
        A1=Kampfgeschwader 53 "Legion Condor"
        A=Maschine 1
        A=Geschwaderstab
Aircraft of the Geschwaderkommodores.

2. Beispiel: He 111 1G+BC
        1G=Kampfgeschwader 27 "Boelke"
        B=Maschine 2
        C=Stab II. Gruppe

3. Beispiel: Fw 200 F8+EH
        F8=Kampfgeschwader 40
        E=Maschine 5
        H=1.Staffel

The identification key for bomber groups, general system and exceptions, in relation to the number of groups.

A=Geschwaderstab (before a blue character)
B=Stab I. Gruppe (before a green character)
C=Stab II. Gruppe (dito)

D=Stab III. Gruppe (same)
E=Stab IV. Gruppe (same)
F=Stab V. Gruppe (same)

I. Gruppe (white)
H=1. Staffel (white)
K=2. Staffel (red)
L=3. Staffel (yellow)

II. Gruppe
M=4. Staffel (white)
N=5. Staffel (red)
P=6. Staffel (yellow)

III. Gruppe (yellow)
R= 7. Staffel (white)
S= 8. Staffel (red)
T= 9. Staffel (yellow)

IV. Gruppe (blue)
U= 10. Staffel (white)
V= 11. Staffel (red)
W= 12. Staffel (yellow)

V. Gruppe
X= 13. Staffel (white)
Y= 14. Staffel (red)
Z= 15. Staffel (yellow)

The letter G, I, J and Q were not used, to prevent confusion.

Planned aircraft allocation of the bomber wings.

Geschwaderstab and Gruppenstab je
3 Flugzeuge

Gruppenstab I. and Staffel 1-3 3+36 Flugzeuge	Gruppenstab II. and Staffel 4-6 3+36 Flugzeuge	Gruppenstab III. and Staffel 7-9 3+36 Flugzeuge

St.1.	St.2.	St.3.	St.4.	St.5.	St.6.	St.7.	St.8.	St.9
12	12	12	12	12	12	12	12	12

This list is only for general example. Some Geschwadern had four or five groups. Sometimes additional Staffeln were also assigned to the Geschwader, for example a 13. Staffel KG 2 and KG 40 were the only to have a fifth Gruppe and this Gruppe was a pure destroyer formation. Exceptions to these rules were often found and this listing should be used as a general guide for the interested reader. This identification form was used by all units with exception of fighter units, close support units and destroyer formations.

In Fall 1941 Winfried Kaiser of 3./LG 1 had his personal emblem painted on the nose of his Ju 88A. It shows a shield with three stars. Also recognizable are the open radiator flaps and the open bottom hatch with extended ladder.

Towards the end of 1943 3./LG 1 was transferred to Patras, Greece. The Ju 88As of this Staffel are painted on their upper sides with the so-called meander pattern, a camouflage frequently used for missions in the Mediterranean area.

...ong range drop-tanks underwing, made an intermediate landing at Reggio-
...r flight from Munich-Riem to Catania.

...m Catania to Tripoli to support the Afrikakorps who were in serious trouble
... flying back to Catania, the tanks of L1+GN are partially emptied.

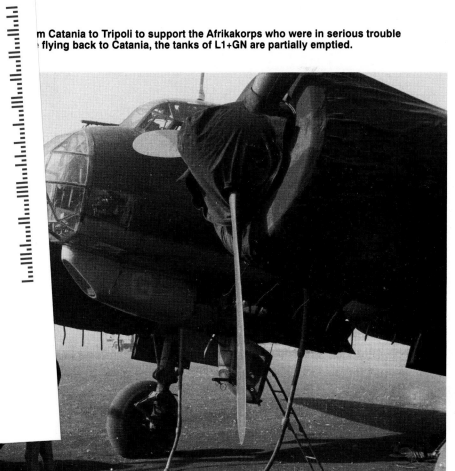

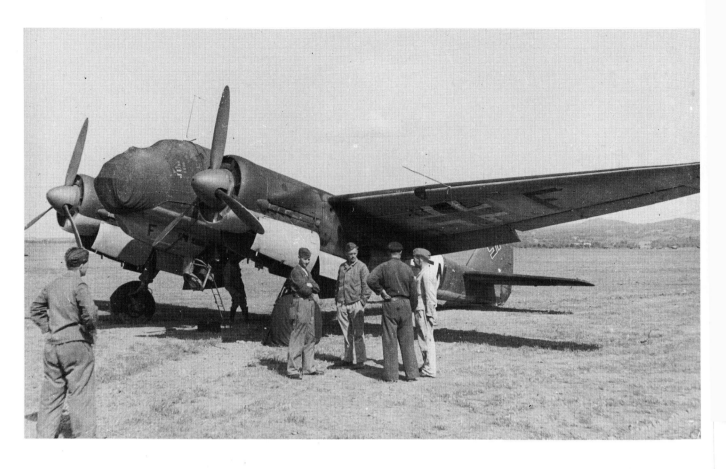

These two photos taken in short sequence show the same Ju 88 L1+FN of 5./LG 1 on May 10, 1941 at Catania. The first photo was taken after its force-landing with retracted tail-wheel due to hits by enemy "Kitty Hawks." Later an Italian aircraft landed and while taxiing collided with the Ju 88A and tore off its rudder. On the underside of the bottom gondola appears the Staffel code letter. The mainwheel tires are covered to prevent damage by heat and solar radiation.

In spring 1942 10./LG 1 at Saloniki-Sedes used concrete bombs for bomb training. For better identification of the machines from the ground, a big number was painted on the rudder. L1+OU displays "14" as can be clearly seen.

After a fighter-bomber attack on the airfield Wiener-Neustadt in spring 1944, not much is left of this Ju 88A with white spiral spinners. It probably belonged to IV./LG 1.

A very nice in flight photo of a He 177A, V4+CP of 6./KG 1. This machine has the meander camouflage all over. The He 177 was conceived as a four-engine bomber with two engines driving one propeller each. This system constantly caused engine trouble and frequently the engines caught fire. Only the normal four-engine versions (one propeller per engine) proved free of trouble. By then it was already too late for series production and therefore it saw very limited combat action.

This photo is full of riddles: it is still unclear as to what unit this He 177A belongs. According to the photographer's statement is belongs to 13./KG 1. The large number 74 on the rudder hint that it could be a training aircraft.

With reference to the Geschwader emblem, KG 3 was called the "Lightning Wing." The machines of all its Gruppen displayed it –the lightning on a shield painted in the respective Gruppe color. This Ju 88A of I./KG 3 with winter camouflage has the shield in white. This photo was taken in winter 1942/43 at Schatalowka, Russia.

These two white camouflaged Ju 88As of I./KG 3 came too close to each other. This collision happened in winter 1942/43 at the airfield of either Charkow or Orel. The machine to the right seems to be coded 5K+MK and belongs to 2./KG 3. Note that the propeller blades are painted white.

This pre-war photo of a He 111B of KG 26 gives the impression of idyllic calmness. All three Gruppen of this Geschwader used the "Lion" emblem with the inscription "Vestigium Leonis" on different colored shields, white, red, or yellow – one color for each Gruppe.

At the turn of the years 1939-1940, 1./KG 26 was stationed at Lübeck Blankensee. From there several missions to Scapa Flow were flown, with Haupt. Martin Vetter (Knight's Cross on May 16, 1940 when Major) as Staffelkapitän. Vetter also initiated a Staffel emblem, as seen here painted on the inner side of the starboard engine. It shows a dwarf sitting on a falling bomb holding a flag(?) in his hand. Beneath it is Vetter's favorite saying: "Zwerg Zaus Dürrer," which he used whenever annoyed.

Combat mission of 5./KG 26 over the North African theater of operations. In this photo is a He 111H coded 1H+EN.

Frequently combat missions came to tragic endings for the crew. On April 24, 1943 this He 111 H of 5./KG 26, code 1H+GN, ditched offshore the Sardinia East coast near Arbatax for unknown reasons.

During the Polish campaign in September 1939, Willi Asmus, a bomb technician with the technical company of KG 27, is busy priming the mechanical fuses of 10-kg bombs in clusters of four each before being stowed in the bomb bay of a He 111.

When attacking industrial targets in England, the steel cables hanging down from barrage balloons were quite a problem. They forced the bomber formations to approach considerably higher thereby losing a great deal of their accuracy. To avoid this, a He 111H-8 was equipped with a cable-cutting device: a balloon cable fender featuring large girder-like structures projecting from beneath the fuselage nose. When hitting it, the cables should be pushed aside and sheared-off at the wing ends. The additional weight of approximately 250 kg had to be balanced by a counterweight at the rear of the fuselage. Since this whole set-up reduced the maneuverability and the bombload considerably, it was discontinued and the machines were re-equipped for glider towing. The picture shows one of those test machines of 1./KG 27 in fall 1940 at Tours.

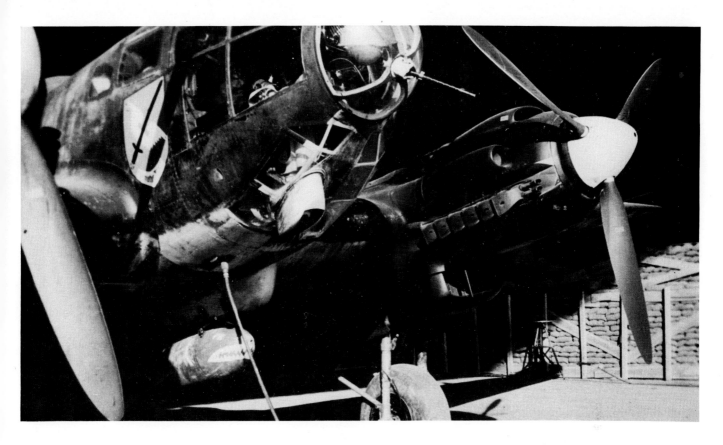

Another picture of a He 111H of 1./KG 27 in fall of 1940 at Tours. Beneath the cockpit is the winged sword, Geschwader emblem of KG 27. Note also the bomb under the fuselage with the sharkmouth painted on it.

A He 111H of 1./KG 27 at the airfield of Tours, has its engines test-run prior to the next sortie to England in fall, 1940. Under the fuselage is a container for incendiary bombs. Thirty-two of the 3-kg stick-type bombs are in each of the eight container chambers.

The latest versions of the He 111H were equipped with a dorsal revolving cupola as defensive armament. This 1./KG 27 aircraft with its carefully painted meander-pattern camouflage is shown here on the airfield of Tarnowitz-Udetfeld in summer 1944. Its underside is painted black for night missions.

Pilot Edo Blohm of 1./KG 30, with a Ju 88A of the Geschwaderstab at Banak, Norway. With reference to its emblem, this unit was called the "Eagle" Geschwader. Its three Gruppen displayed this emblem in a shield with the respective Gruppe color: red, white or yellow.

Edo Blohm obviously was fond of being photographed with his aircraft. This Ju 88A belongs to I./KG 30. The photo was taken presumably in spring 1941 in Parchim. Comparing this photo with that on the bottom of page 186, the different types of bottom gondolas can be noted.

According to Blohm's statement, this bomb-carrying stork was the Staffel emblem of 12./KG 30.

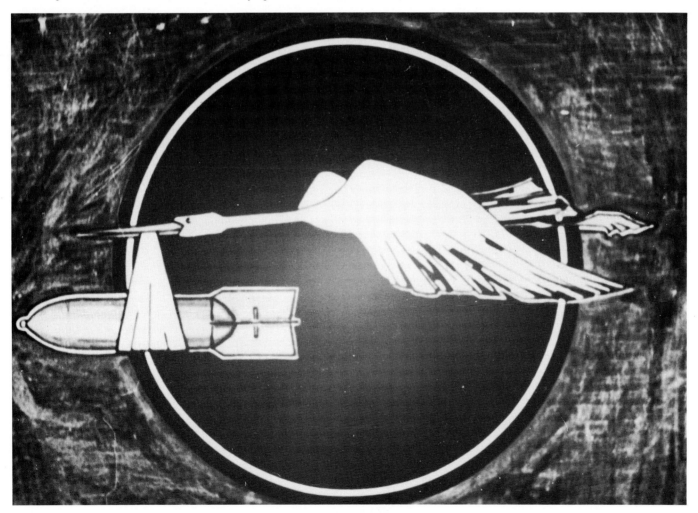

These two photos show 4D+GM of 4./KG 30, and were taken on March 10, 1943 in Lister, Norway. Note the black painted upper areas of the aircraft, the overpainted national insignias and the exhaust flame dampers. In the nose is a 20mm MG/FF cannon.

At the beginning of the war KG 40 was the only combat unit equipped with the four-engine Fw 200 "Condor", the military conversion of the civil airliner "Kurier." With these aircraft I./KG 40 flew armed reconnaissance missions over the Atlantic as far as Iceland. This Fw 200C of I. Gruppe was photographed in spring 1941 at Stavanger-Sola Land (Norway). Parked in the background is a Do 17, coded 4N+KK of 2./Aufkl.Gr.22.

Shown here is a Fw 200C during engine maintenance in a I./KG 40 hangar, and requiring three different types of ladders. Seen beneath the cockpit is the emblem of I./KG 40, the globe with Saturn ring.

"Schweinsgeige" (pig-violin) on a 88A rudder does not indicate, as could be assumed, to instrument flying school 2 at Neubiberg. This actually was the Staffel emblem of KG 51, which was initiated by its Staffelkapitän, Oblt. von Wenschowski, who was killed in action on July 7, 1941 after a sortie with SD-2 bombs.

This photo of a III./KG 51 Ju 88A was taken at Balti, Russia in September 1941, and shows some interesting details. Easily recognizable is the sighting device of the MG 81/7.9mm on the forward part of the cockpit.

Lt. Kielhorn finally brought his "Mühle" ("crate," or "heap") home. This photo of a Ju 88A of III./KG 51 was taken in summer 1941 in Russia. Unclear is the meaning of the numbers 49 and 5249497 beside the edelweiss emblem on the nose. The seven-digit number could be the Werknummer of the manufacturer.

Inappropriately camouflaged for winter missions was this He 111H code A1+BT, WNr. 4566, of 9./KG 53 "Legion Condor." Noticeable besides the MG/FF 20mm in the nose, is the single ETC (external bomb rack) with SC 1000-kg bomb.

Good in-flight photos of the Ju 88S series are very rare. This Ju 88 S-1, RF+MR, belongs to I./KG 66 and still displays the factory-applied splinter camouflage. Underwing, close to the "R" is the antenna of the electrical precision altimeter FuG 101a. This device was radar-based, and was extremely precise, even in the 0-3 meter range, compared to the previously used barometric altimeters.

In the summer of 1944 on the airfield of Montdidier, France, pilot Friedlieb Blauert, I./KG 66, parked his Ju 188E on the taxiway. A strange sight is the dapple-pattern camouflage, when compared to the usual meander pattern. The national insignia are totally covered.

Above, below and opposite top: Three photos of Lt. Hans Altrogge's Ju 88S-1, code Z6+BH, of I./KG 66, taken in 1944. In the top photo the aircraft's upper areas still display the mottle pattern, while the lower photo shows repair spots on the nose and on the upper part of the rudder. This was necessary after damages received during a pathfinder mission over England. This unit was activated especially as route- and target-markers for bomber formations and proved very successful.

Below: To extend the range of this Ju 88S-3 of I./KG 66, drop-tanks were fixed under wings and fuselage. In March/April 1945 these aircraft also flew pathfinder missions for the "Mistelgespanne" of KG 30 to destroy the bridges crossing the Oder river. Remarkable are the complete and intensive camouflage of the aircraft at the undersides and the drop-tanks and the open radiator flaps of the right Jumo 213 engine.

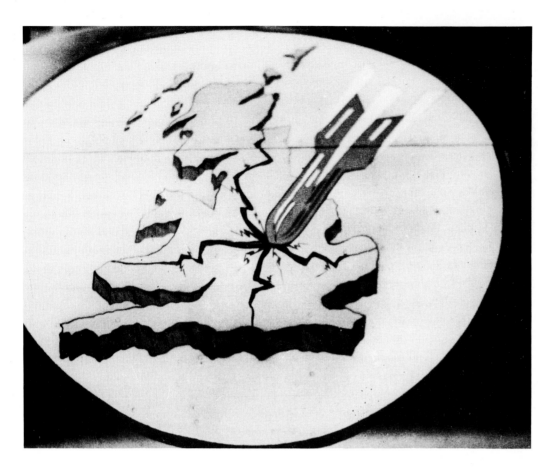

The England-smashing bomb or
17Z in the summer of 1940 was t
emblem of 3./KG 76. For the wea
German bomber formations an
optimistic emblem!

In the summer of 1940 this emblem
was used at 9./KG 76. There was also
an emblem with three offset and
upward-pointing arrows in the shield
of this Staffel.

Interesting Do 17Z cockpit details at KG 76. Besides the three MG 17/7.9mm, the guiding cams are clearly visible. They are adjusted to avoid hitting parts of the own aircraft while firing. Note also the lenticular MG mount, the antenna mast and the double-loop antenna.

153, activated in Merseburg, cted the thievish magpie as its ope emblem. After re-designation KG 77 in Spring 1939 the emblem maintained for some time. In the ground is 3Z+EK of 2./KG 77. On nose immediately below the "E" faintly discernible is Do 17E-3, . 2049.

Ju 88 of Stab I./KG 77 lined up for parade on the airfield at Dno during the beginning of the Russian campaign. Remarkable are the light colored spinners.

Most successful at anti-shipping missions was KG 77's Johannes Geisman. Scored on his rudder are twelve vessels, sunk or damaged (the mark V near the silhouette stands for sunk, B for damaged), and his first air victory on October 4, 1942 in the Mediterranean theater. Geismann was awarded the Knight's Cross on December 21, 1942.

This Ju 88A, code 7T+FH of 1./KGR 606, is shown approaching targets in the Mediterranean theater. The successful pilot with the remarkable score is unknown. Beginning in September 1942 KGr. 606 was redesignated I./KG 77, while the previous I./KG 77 was redesignated I./KG 6 at the end of August.

Sicily, September 1942. This Ju 88A of I./KG 77 is refilled with oil. When KGr. 606 was redesignated I./KG 77, the Hahn-emblem was retained. It was initiated by the former Kommandeur of KGr. 606, Joachin Hahn. Hahn was awarded the Knight's Cross on October 21, 1940. He was killed in action on June 3, 1942.

A very unusually camouflaged Bf 109G, 3Z+?B, flew with I./KG 77. It may have been used for liaison and communications, but it is unknown whether it was also used for escort missions or whether victories in it were achieved. In the cockpit is the Oberwerkmeister of 1./KG 77 (Oberwerkmeister was an NCO-rank, comparable with the U.S. chief warrant officer; precondition for his rank was a master's degree as aero-engine mechanic).

In early Summer 1944, I./KG 77 based at Salon en Provence flew sorties against convoys in the Mediterranean Sea. For easier take-off when loaded with heavy torpedoes, they used so-called R-Gerate (solid-fuel rockets), which when burned-out were dropped, parachuted and re-used. Note the all-over meander camouflage. One exception is shown in the photo: a presumably brand-new Ju 88A/LT still displaying the factory code (Werkskennung). On July 20, 1944 I./KG 77 was redesignated I.KG 26.

This beautiful In flight picture of a Do 17E, code 3Z+A? of Stab II./KG 77 demonstrates the effect of the segment camouflage seen for higher altitudes. This photo was taken around 1939-1940.

After take-off at Comiso, Sicily in spring 1942, this heavy laden Ju 88A of 4./KG 77 is approaching Malta. Under the fuselage a heavy bomb is recognizable. Note how exhaust fumes sooted the upper wing areas aft of the engines.

In July/August 1943, I. and II./KG 77 were transferred from Italy and East-Prussia for re-equipping to Ju 88A/LTs (aerial torpedo versions). A line of Ju 88, probably belonging to II./KG 77 is shown here. Note the two white rings on the spinners and the tube shaped sights of the rearward MGs.

Ju 88A/LTs of 5./KG 77 are loaded with practice torpedoes, recognizable by the two-colored nose. They are shown here during reequipping to torpedo bombers in July/August 1943. Note 3Z+KN being loaded. Note the square torpedo rudders.

Ready for a night mission against targets in England is this Ju 88A of II./KG 77 on the airfield of Rennes, France in June 1942. The undersides of fuselage and wings are painted with a washable black camouflage paint.

After a low-altitude attack in 1941 this Ju 88A of 9./KG 77, code 3Z+FT, landed with considerable damage in the area of Aieverskaja, Russia. During the attack the oxygen cylinder in the fuselage was hit by an enemy shell and exploded.

Right and opposite below: Interesting what ingenuity creates within the units to improve the armament of the aircraft. Pilot Günther Wagner of III./KG 77 equipped his Ju 88A with an additional MG 17/7.9mm in the nose beside the 20mm cannon MG/FF. It was mounted just above the window for the sight and the cartridge ejector guide in front of it. Note the ammunition beltfeed emptying the cockpit towards the ventral gondola. The bomb sight was probably not used, since by this time the unit was flying strafing missions only.

KG 100 was the first real target finder of the Luftwaffe, as its first and main missions were in 1940-1941 during the air battles over Britain. The unit's first big success in target marking was during the attack on Coventry. This photo shows a test-run of a 2./KGr.100 He 111H's engines in the winter of 1940-1941 at Vannes, France. The underside of the machine has a washable black finish.

Prior to KGr.100's transfer to Russia in August 1941, the black camouflage paint at the aircraft's underside had to be washed off.

Propeller cleaners and their "Dora", a He 177A of II./KG 100 at Aalborg-West, presumably in late summer-fall 1944. Here the size of the mighty four-bladed propellers is impressively shown. Each propeller is driven by two DB 610 engines in twin arrangement, producing 2950 hp. Note the meander camouflage and the outlined sheet metal joints.

This Do 17E belonged to the so-called Alpengeschwader (Mountain-Wing) I./KG 255 before the unit was re-equipped with Do 17Zs. This aircraft was re-coded NG+PI and transferred to FFS C 7 Finsterwalde (C-class pilot school). The Staffel emblem remained on its nose, also the name "Habicht" (Hawk). Note also the forward ringsight in front of the windshield.

This rare photo shows Do 17Z of I./
KGr.606 in April 1940 at Copenhagen,
Denmark. 2.(F) Ku.Fl.Gr. after several
reconnaissance missions over the
Northsea, was redesignated in
November 1939 to I/KGr.606, and
consisted of three Staffeln equipped
with He 111s. In April 1940 the He 111s
were turned-in for new Do 17Zs.

This photo was also taken in April
1940 at Copenhagen after re-
equipping to Do 17Zs. Note the shield
depicting an eagle over England and
Ireland, which was the emblem of
KGr.606. It was replaced by the Hahn-
emblem later the same year.

This Do 17, coded U4+QH, of an as yet unknown unit, was photographed at Krefeld in May 1940. The letter "H" denotes that it is the 1. Staffel in its Geschwader.

The same story with this Do 17Z, though its unit is not certain, it could be KG 76. The emblem depicts a bomb over a snow-covered hill.

This Do 17P, crash-landed during the campaign in France and displays the code Z5+?? of an as yet unidentified unit. It could possibly be a reconnaissance group.

This photo of a He 111H is quite a puzzle. It was taken in spring 1940 on the Greifswald airbase just prior to the Norwegian campaign. Note the unknown winged bomb emblem, and the lack of defensive weapons.

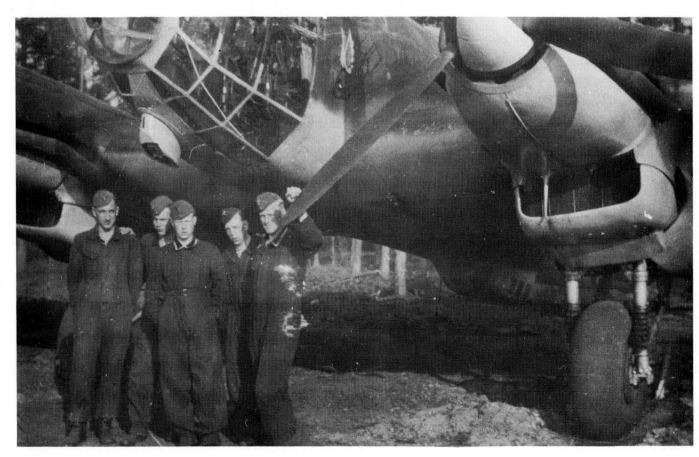

Around the turn of the year 1942/43, III./KG 76 selected the city emblem of Heidelberg as its Gruppe emblem, honoring its Kommandeur Haupt. Heinrich Schweickhard (Knight's Cross on February 4, 1942, Oak Leaves on December 30, 1942) and his hometown. Note the sliding cockpit window and the name-plate beneath the "8."

The sixth test model of the He 177, coded BC+BP, WNr. 00006, at Neubrandenburg. In August 1942 test models V6 and V7 joined IV./ KG 40 at Bordeaux-Merignac for combat trials. The results were very satisfactory.

In April/May 1941 the delivery of Ju 88A-4s to operational units had started. The A-4 was built in greater quantities than any other Ju 88 version. It differed from its predecessor, the Ju 88A-5 mainly in its engines, the 1410 hp Jumo 211. Note in the photo that DE+JX is painted sand brown. Also note the rearward defense armament, two MG 81/7.9mm guns.

This Ju 88A from Wassenaar, Holland, is shown here after landing in at Fürsty airbase in the winter of 1944. As can be seen by the exhaust flame dampers on the engines, it was surely also used for night missions. The unit is unknown.

The Ju 88 C was a heavy fighter or destroyer (Zerstörer), and was derived from the A-5 bomber version. Instead of the nose glazing it had three MG 17/7.9mm, and three MG 151/20mm guns in the nose and the ventral gondola producing very effective fire power. The aircraft in these two photos, taken in the fall of 1942 at Tatzinskaja, Russia, had false glazing painted on the nose, to make it look like a bomber. To the left of this fake glazing are the cartridge ejector slots for the MG 17. This aircraft could possibly be of 7.(Eis.)/ KG 51 which was equipped with this type in spring 1942.

These remarkably camouflaged Ju 88s could possibly belong to III./KG 54. The wave pattern camouflage was frequently used by units with anti-shipping missions. These photos were probably taken in the Mediterranean area towards the end of 1942.

Chapter VII

Stuka and Close-Support Units

The following is a list of the most important units:

Stukaverbände
St.G.1
St.G.2
St.G.3
St.G.5
St.G.51
St.G.76
St.G.77
I.(St)/186(T)
IV.(St)/LG 1

Schnellkampfverbände
SKG 10
SKG 210

Nachtschlachtverbände
NSG 1-12
NSG 20
NSG 30

Ostfliegertaffel Russia
Behelfskampfstaffel Luftflotte 1
Behelfskampfstaffel Luftwaffenkommando Ost
Störkampfgruppe Luftwaffenkommando Ost
Störkampfgruppe Luftwaffenkommando Südost
Störkampfgruppe Luftflotte 4

Schlachtverbände
SG 1
SG 2
SG 3
SG 4
SG 5
SG 9
SG 10
SG 77
SG 101
SG 102
SG 103
SG 111
SG 151

In June 1938 Fliegergruppe 50 was activated at Lechfeld and equipped with the Hs 123A ground-attack aircraft. This photo shows the 50+?? displaying the black triangle, then the marking for ground-attack aircraft, and the Staffel emblem, which was later adopted by 9./St.G.2. On November 1, 1938 Fliegergruppe 50 was redesignated II./St.G.162, and on May 1, 1939 finally designated III./St.G.2.

Some of the most unusual "paint art" we've seen on German aircraft is shown here in the summer of 1938 at 3./Fliegergruppe 50. A Hs 123A was painted especially for Lt. Hamann, the Gruppenadjutant. His formation taught him flying in his off-time as he never attended flying school! Heinrich Brucker, the Staffelkapitän of the 3. Staffel looks somewhat morose, while Lt. Hamann (on wing) seems to feel pretty well. Hamann was killed during the French campaign when a flak shell hit his Ju 87B.

This photo shows 10. St./LG 1 aircraft in spring 1940 over the Norwegian hills returning from a sortie. One 300 liter drop tank is fixed under each wing of the Ju 87R, which is the long range version of the "B"-type.

During the French campaign in spring 1940, this Hs 123A, WNr. 2434, coded L2+LM of 4.(S)/LG 2, crash landed near Nevers, France for unknown reasons. The "Mickey Mouse" painting was later made the Gruppe emblem.

The Berlin-bear with ax was the Staffel emblem of 5.(S)/LG 2, and is clearly visible on this Hs 123A, coded L2+HN, shown here ready for take-off at Krefeld-Uerdingen towards the beginning of 1940.

During the Balkan campaign in the spring of 1941, this Ju 87B/R, coded A5+HH, of 1./St.G.1 taxies to its takeoff position passing the Gruppe flag. Note that the engine cowling and entire rear of the aircraft is painted in a lighter color. This photo was probably taken at Krajnici, Romania towards the beginning of the campaign.

After a strafing attack on the North African field airstrip of I./St.G.1 in 1941, this burned-out wreck was all that remained of a Ju 87B. Visible under the fuselage is the loose-hanging bomb crutch.

Two mechanics are busy with a Ju 87B of the Geschwaderstab of St.G.2 "Immelmann." On the engine cowling is the Stab emblem, the escutcheon with the white cross. The domestic duck waddling leisurely on the wing is the mascot of 7./St.G.2!

Engine change at a Ju 87R of Geschwaderstab St.G.2. in spring 1941 at the Krajnini, Romania airstrip. At left, standing on the ladder, is the TO of 7./St.G.2, Lt. Armin Thiede, inspecting the Jumo 211 D. Thiede was awarded the Knight's Cross on June 14, 1941. He died in an accident on July 9, 1941 in Ostrice near Varasdin, Croatia. Together with several other soldiers he was a passenger in a DFS 230 cargo glider, when a wing collapsed and the glider crashed to the ground.

Another engine change, this time on a Ju 87B of III./St.G.2 at Norvenich, towards the beginning of May 1940, just prior to the French campaign. This aircraft has the 1210 hp Jumo 211 engine. The large ventral radiator with its cooling gills was typical for this version.

Deceptive peace at the III./St.G.2 airstrip at Krajnici, Romania in spring 1941. On the first four Ju 87Rs the Teutonic Order cross can be seen, the emblem of the Geschwaderstab aircraft of St.G.2. Further three holders of the Knight's Cross: far right Oblt. Dieter Pekrun, Geschwaderadjutant; third from right sitting and with raised arm Haupt. Heinrich Brücker, Kommandeur of III./St.G.2, and sitting in front off him Haupt. Günther Schwärzel, Staffelkapitän of 9./St.G.2. All three were awarded the Knight's Cross on June 24, 1941.

Even Haupt. Heinrich Brücker, Kommandeur of III./St.G.2 sometimes had bad luck. On April 11, 1941 after a maintenance trial flight and landing at Krajnici, a sod of grass jammed the landing gear and caused the Ju 87R with its 300 liter drop tanks to nose over.

Another photo of the nose-over of Haupt. Heinrich Brücker's, Ju 87R on April 11, 1941 on the Krajnici airstrip. Clearly visible is the emblem of III. Gruppe, a patriarch cross, the treads near the wing roots and the dive sirens on the undercarriage legs.

Waiting for the signal for take-off is this Fw 190A at the airfield of Graz in Spring 1944. Note the unusual camouflage finish with straight line pattern, and the missing code at the fuselage. This aircraft could possibly belong to I./SG 4.

Reporting to the Kommandeur of SG 4 is Heinrich Brücker (above photo far right) at Graz in Spring 1944. Note the filled-in metal sheet joints, and the starter cart.

The crews of Geschwaderstab SG 77 prepare for their next sortie at Lemberg, 1944. During this period the Stab was equipped with Ju 87D-5s with extended wing spans. The wing code S2+ appears in reduced size within the yellow fuselage band.

Loading the wing MG 151/20mm of a Ju 87D of Geschwaderstab SG 77. Note that the abbreviation SG 77 is used instead of St.G.77. This is explained by the fact, that effective October 18, 1943 most Stukageschwadern were renamed ground-attack or close-support wings. Along with this organization went the increased re-equipping to Fw 190s.

During 1944, the partial re-equipping of the Stuka units from Ju 87s to Fw 190s was continued, including the Geschwaderstab of SG 77 at Reichshof, Poland. In this photo a mechanic is warming up the "E" of the Geschwader-Ia.

Reichshof, Poland, 1944. The Geschwader-Ia's aircraft is test run before take-off for the next strafing mission. Note the bomb load on this Fw 190: a so-called Dinort stick is screwed into the bomb tip, acting as a percussion fuze, which causes the bomb to detonate just before hitting the ground, whereby fragmentation is increased considerably. This type of bomb was used primarily against troop concentrations and unarmed vehicles.

A "proud Cock" was selected by 4./St.G.77 as their Staffel emblem. This photo of a Ju 87B was taken in 1940 during the French campaign. Not that underwing and at the undercarriage legs the letter "K" of the unit code has been applied.

A very worn Ju 87B of 4./St.G.77 with winter camouflage. The high grade of FWT (fair, wear & tear) decreased the combat-readiness of the Staffel considerably.

Until the beginning of 1940 5./St.G.77 had a mule in its Staffel emblem. All Staffeln of St.G.77 had the same type of shield, only the upper serrated part showed the respective Staffel color.

With the beginning 1944 5./St.G.77 replaced its old mule emblem with a new panther emblem. This remained until the end of the war. Seen here is a Ju 87B, WNr. 5235, coded S2+DN.

An honor formation flying over the Ju 87B "Heinz Bumke" code F1+AM, of Haupt. Otto Schmidt, Staffelkapitän of 7./St.G.77, on the occasion of his completing 500 missions on August 28, 1942. Note the unit code denotes this aircraft to II./KG 76 with the "M" of 4. Staffel, while the fuselage displays the emblem of 7./St.G.77. Heinze Bumke was a Staffelkapitän with III./St.G.77 until his death, but his name did not fall into oblivion, as can be seen on the engine cowling. In the photo below is Otto Schmidt with his radio operator in front of his aircraft. After 527 missions, Schmidt was awarded the Knight's Cross on September 3, 1942.

This Ju 87B, coded F1+BM, of 7./St.G.77, is loaded with bombs and is on the way to its target. The letter "B" in its code, which denotes where the machine is placed within the Staffel, appears additionally on the landing gear spats.

7. and 8./St.G.77 aircraft returning from a sortie against Sevastopol in June-July 1942. Note the different placement of the fuselage bands.

The diving eagle was the unit emblem of 9./St.G.77. The location shown in this photo is Fleis, in northern France on July 12, 1940. This aircraft also displays the letter "A" of its code on the wheelspats.

In every Geschwader or operational formation, IV. Gruppe was assigned the task of training new pilots for combat. Here is a photo of a Ju 87B of 10./St.G.77 loaded with concrete bombs. Besides the escutcheon with the squirrel, we see the high number "25" on the wheel spats. Such high numbers were used by training units.

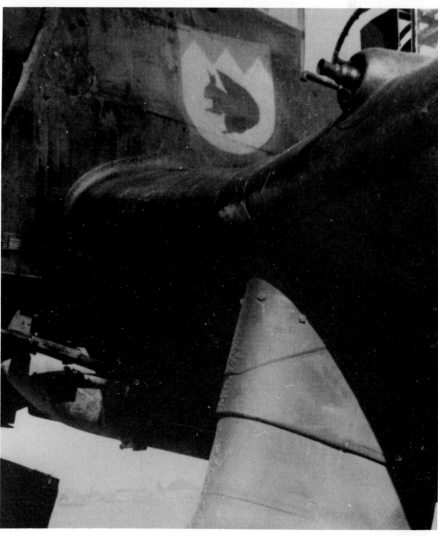

This Hs 129B with Mk 101 cannon in a weapons pod under the fuselage belongs to 10.(Pz)/JG 51. In September 1943 this unit was redesignated 14.(Pz)/SG 9. As a tank destroyer, this aircraft was armed with four MG 151/20mm guns, and one 30mm cannon in its nose. The aircraft shown here is the early B-2 version. The left side opening on the nose is an air inlet for the weapons hydraulic cylinder, and to the right is an automatic camera for photographing ground attacks.

This is a very rare photo: A Ju 87D-7 with exhaust flame dampers and a new weapons arrangement of two MG 151/20mm guns in the wings. The aircraft was coded 1K+IK and belonged to 2./NSGr.4.

Russian U-2 biplanes appeared almost every night over German lines and were more of a nuisance to the infantry for disturbing their rest rather that their aimless bombing. In 1942 as a countermeasure, German nuisance radar units were activated and included various types of aircraft. In October 1943 they were renamed to Nachtschlachtgruppen (nocturnal ground attack units). Shown here is a Go 145 of NSGr.4 loaded with Russian 100 kg bombs on its way to a target.

Assigned to NSGr.11 were also Fw 58C. Out of the ordinary is the code VW+3W, instead VW+VE, as was usual.

The Luftwaffe trial group for carrier landings, August 1943 at Perugia, Italy included this Ju 87B, code SH+OB, shown over mountainous territory. Clearly visible at the tailwheel is the arrester hook used by carrier-based aircraft.

Another very rare specimen within the Luftwaffe is this Ju 87D with skis. Its unit is unknown. Note how the skis are mounted, simply by taking the wheel off of the undercarriage leg and mounting the ski in its place.

CHAPTER VIII

Transport Units of the Luftwaffe

Unit Markings

Due to the use of KGr.z.b.V. for the newly formed paratroop units, the general unit of organization was altered. To fulfill the requirements of a paratrooper battalion, which consisted of a Stab and four companies, a KGr.z.b.V. consisted from this time on of a Stabschwarm with four or five other Staffeln of twelve aircraft each. The combat units z.b.V. consisted of four Gruppen of the same components and a Geschwaderstab with five aircraft. The only real KGr.z.b.V. was designated 1. All others were called KGr.z.b.V. until May 1943 where they were reorganized to Transportgeschwadern.

A = Geschwaderstab (before a blue letter)
B = Stab I. Gruppe
C = Stab II. Gruppe
D = Stab III. Gruppe
E = Stab IV. Gruppe

I.-IV. Gruppe (before a green letter)

I. Gruppe (white)
H = 1. Staffel (white)
K = 2. Staffel (red)
L = 3. Staffel (yellow)
M = 4. Staffel (blue)

II. Gruppe (white)
N = (5) 1. Staffel (white)
P = (6) 2. Staffel (red)
R = (7) 3. Staffel (yellow)
S = (8) 4. Staffel (blue)

III. Gruppe (white)
T = (9) 1. Staffel (white)
U = (10) 2. Staffel (red)
V = (11) 3. Staffel (yellow)
W = (12) 4. Staffel (blue)

IV. Gruppe (white)
X = (13) 1. Staffel (white)
Y = (14) 2. Staffel (red)
Z = (15) 3. Staffel (yellow)
Q = (16) 4. Staffel (white)

J = (17) 1. Staffel (white)

Tactical markings of Transportgruppen

Often Transportgruppen were developed by high command through the necessity of mission requirements. This means that aircraft required for specific missions were brought together from different transport commands and then upon completion of the mission returned to their original units. Aircraft assigned for a specific mission received special markings and returned these markings upon returning to their original units. This subsequently led to chaos within the units in respect to visual identification which seemed to have no pattern whatsoever. To regain control of the identification system, KGr.z.b.V.400 in fall 1941, in Russia, implemented a new system which assumed visual order within a Gruppe. This new system was the basis for the later tactical identification system that was so important.

How does the tactical marking system look?

Example:
P4   P = Major Pfister, Kommandeur of KGr.z.b.V.400
K   4 = 4. Staffel of the Gruppe
       K = aircraft "K" of the Staffel, also aircraft 11

One can see that these markings resemble the same information as the normal fuselage side markings. The only problem is the first letter.

Transport groups that proved to carry tactical markings

T.Kz.	Unit	Code	Gruppen-bzw Staffelbuchstaben
B	KGr.z.b.V.500	J6	B, H, K, L, M
D	IV./KG.z.b.V.1	1Z	F, X, Y, Z, Q
H	KGr.z.b.V.106 (to May 1943 III./TG2)	4V	C, N, P, R, S
K	Kampfgruppe Major Kupschus (1941 Russia)	-	-
K	KGr.z.b.V.Frankfurt (Nov.1942-March 1943)	-	-
N	I./KGr.z.b.V.172 (to May 1943 IV./TG 3)	4V	D, T, U, V, W
P	KGr.z.b.V.400 (P then T.Kz. to Nov.1942)	4F	A, B, C, D, E
P	III./TG 1	1Z	D, T, U, V, W
S	Lufttransportstaffel (See) 222	X4	H
T	KGr.z.b.V.800 (to May 1943 I./TG 3)	-	-
W	KGr.z.b.V. Wittstock (Nov.1942-March 1943)	-	-
W	Lufttransportstaffel (See) 1	G 6/8 A	J
X	II./KGr.z.b.V.323 (to may 1943 I./TG 5)	C8	B, E, F, G
Y	II./KGr.z.b.V.323	C8	C, N, P, R, S
Z	III./KG.z.b.V1	1Z	D, T, U, V, W
Z	Savoiastaffel d. III./KG.z.b.V.1 (to May 1943 Transportstaffel IV. Fliegerkorps)	1Z	D

This list is by no means complete, and we are sure there are more unknown markings. In may 1943, all Transportgruppen were redesignated as Transportgeschwadern and their tactical markings disappeared. Even after the change there were still exceptions. The aircraft allocation of TG 5, equipped with Me 323s, differed completely from the normal organization. Each Gruppe consisted of one Stabstaffel and three Staffeln with six Me 323s each, totaling twenty-four aircraft.

Intense activity on a North African airstrip in November 1942. The Ju 52/3m, code 1Z+BH, belongs to 1./KG.z.b.V.1, as can be seen by the fuselage marking and the very important tactical number "1 2" on the rudder. Only by this tactical number the aircraft can be definitely assigned to a certain unit. A KGr.z.b.V. is a temporary formation, consisting of aircraft especially suited for a particular mission and recruited from different Luftwaffe units. They retained their original codes, but for identification within the new unit they were assigned tactical numbers painted on both sides of the rudder.

In very loose formation, Ju 52/3ms Africa bound over the Mediterranean. In the foreground are two machines of 6./KG.z.b.V.1, 1Z+DP, and 1Z+CP. To explain their coding: the "P" and the "6" stand for 6. Staffel, the "C" and "D" denote the third and fourth aircraft within the Staffel. At KG.z.b.V.1 the large number and the next to last letter denote their place within the Staffel.

Supplying Demjansk in February 1942. These Ju 52/3ms of 6./KG.z.b.V. fly low level over vast, snow-covered Russia. The aircraft are partially camouflaged to match the existing winter conditions. These aircraft can be identified only by their tactical numbers on the rudder, while their fuselage coding TG+EB does not give any information about their origin.

After landing within the Demjansk pocket, the Ju 52/3ms of II./KG.z.b.V.1 had to be refuelled by their crews with hand pumps.

During the Demjansk supply missions, the Ju 52/3m transports and their crews were taken from various schools and ordered to Pleskau to activate KG.z.b.V. Second from left is Lt. Paul Temme, an experienced instructor pilot of FFS B5 at Neubrandenburg. Behind the group of officers is a Ju 52 from an instrument-flying school, recognized by its emblem with the "Blind Cow," now with II./KGr.z.b.V.1.

A funny, though regretfully unknown emblem on a Ju 52/3m, seen during the Demjansk supplying. This aircraft while probably flew with II./KGr.z.b.V.1.

This Ju 52/3m possibly belongs to KG.z.b.V.1. Whether the salamander painting is a Staffel emblem or personal badge is unclear. Mounted on the top of the cockpit is an additional cupola for defense.

A suit case carrying angel was the Staffel emblem of 2./KGr.z.b.V.9. This photo of a Ju 52/3m was taken during the Demjansk supply missions of February 1942.

Ground crew mechanics servicing the three Brama 323 engines of a Ju 52/3m of 1./KGr.z.b.V.106 towards the end of April 1940 at Oslo-Fornebu. The umbrella, a personal emblem of pilot Friedlieb Blauert, had its own story: on September 17, 1939 Blauert was a member of 1./KG 26 and participated on a mission against Scapa Flow. During the bomb-run, every crew member also threw an umbrella out of the aircraft, alluding to Prime Minister Neville Chamberlain's umbrella.

Only a few models were built of the Ju 352A, a further development of the legendary Ju 52/3m. It had also three engines, however wood was used for the fuselage and wings instead of corrugated sheet metal. Under the tarp covering the forward part of the fuselage is a weapons cupola. This photo was probably taken around the end of 1944/beginning 1945 in the Magdeburg area. The unit is unknown.

In 1944 the landing strip of Celle-Witzenbruch was obviously too short even for the Ar 232B, nicknamed "Millipede" by the soldiers. The railroad line Celle-Hannover stopped the landing abruptly. The tailunit was a tube-shaped boom protruding from the upper rear part of the fuselage. Beneath the boom root was a hydraulically operated loading door.

The Luftwaffe's most interesting transport aircraft was without a doubt the Arado 232, versions A and B. What made this machine outstanding were the small wheels under the fuselage, which enabled it to land on unprepared areas. Even small ditches could be crossed safely. This photo shows an Ar 232B with four 1000 hp Bramo 323 R-2 engines of an unknown unit in wintry Russia.

In 1943 parts of II./JG 51 were transported to North Africa with this Ju 52/3m. Note the emblem depicts the silhouette of Scandinavia. This unknown emblem may have belonged to a unit which participated in the occupation of Denmark and Norway in 1940.

The impossible sometimes happens: according to a witnesses' statement, this Ju 52/3m landed in Mannhiem in the summer of 1939, which was at this time a pre-war base of I./JG 51. Later during an engine change in 1940 it was found that this aircraft never belonged to I./JG 51, yet no one in that unit missed it! The origin of the emblem is unknown, though it looks considerably Bavarian.

This Me 323D of an unknown transport unit, possibly TG 5, was seen in September 1944 at Memel, Russia. Due to its enormous dimensions, the "Gigant's" huge cargo compartment could accommodate up to twenty-two tons of equipment, or light armored vehicles. The bicycle leaning against the aircraft, shows the Gigant's dimensions.

To get sufficient transport capacity for the Norway campaign, Lufthansa had to assign its Ju 90B airlines to the Luftwaffe. This photo was taken end of April 1940 on the airfield of Oslo-Fornebu. According to the photographer, on May 1, 1940 during an air raid against this airfield, this Ju 90B was destroyed. With its four 750 hp BMW 132 H engines the Ju 90B was underpowered, and had not yet come up to the expectations of Lufthansa.

The Eastern Front also saw the use of Lufthansa Ju 90Bs for transport. In this photo something seems to be wrong with the undercarriage of the "Baden." This photo was taken in the winter of 1942 at Krasnogwardeisk, Russia.

This Ju 52/3m unit seems to have accomplished missions all over Europe. The emblem on the engine cowling leads to this conclusion. However, the unit is unknown.

Laboriously taxiing through deep snow to its take-off point is this Ju 53/3m of LLG 1. Note the rear-view mirror above the canopy and the wing emblem, a green comet with three tails.

Chapter IX

Navy Units of the Luftwaffe

The following is a list of the most important units:

Kü.Fl.Gr. 106
Kü.Fl.Gr. 306
Kü.Fl.Gr. 406
Kü.Fl.Gr. 506
Kü.Fl.Gr. 606
Kü.Fl.Gr. 706
Kü.Fl.Gr. 806
Kü.Fl.Gr. 906

SAGr. 125
SAGr. 126
SAGr. 127
SAGr. 128
SAGr. 129
SAGr. 130
SAGr. 131

1. & 5. Bordfliegerstaffel 106

10./(See) LG 2

Minensuchgruppe der Luftwaffe

Küstenstaffel Krim
Küstenstaffel Ostsee

Fl.Erg.Gr. (See) Kamp

Erp.Staffel 167
Sonderstaffel Transozean

LufttransportGr. (See) 1
Lufttransportstaffel (See) 222

Seenotstaffel 4
Seenotstaffel 5
Seenotstaffel 9
Seenotstaffel 10
Seenotflugkommando 1
Seenotgruppe 81

Heinkel He 59Bs of 3./Ku.Fl.Gr.106 are shown here lined-up in the Kurische Haff near Pillau-Lochstadt, East Prussia. In 1937 this Staffel initiated the escutcheon with the winged sword as unit emblem. The photo was probably shot during this period.

Both of these photos were taken 1937 at the landing ramp of Hornu. General purpose floatplanes test-run their engines while waiting for launching. The aircraft belonged to 3./Ku.Fl.Gr.506 and are coded 60+G53/Y53 and E 53 and display the letters on the nose also. To move the floatplanes to land, they were set on special trolleys, so called slipcarts.

For dawn and night missions the u[n]
sides of this He 115C of 3./Ku.Fl.Gr.
were finished with an uneven camo
pattern. This photo was made in the
of 1941 in Norway. Note the filigree
bracing and the covered engines.

The shield with the ram's head was
emblem of 3./Ku.Fl.Gr.506, as seen
He 115C stationed in Norway in 19

In the harbor at Alborg, Denmark a He 59B of 1./Ku.Fl.Gr.706, armed with three depth charges, waits at a mooring buoy for its next anti-submarine mission in the area of Skagerak on the Baltic Sea. According to the photographer, these seaplanes flew successful missions during World War II, which is the possible time frame for this photo. The emblem of this unit depicts a harpooned shark jumping out of the sea.

Low level formation flight of two Luftwaffe giants of LTS (See) 222 (This was a combat trial unit for V-versions of Bv 222 flying boats only.) This photo shows aircraft V4 coded X4+DH, and V5 coded X4+EH, and was taken in 1942 during a supply mission to North Africa. Beneath the cockpit is the Staffel emblem, a white circle with a viking ship and, on the rudder, the tactical letter "S."

Another photo of Bv 222 V5, LTS 222 (See) in Summer 1942 taken either in the harbor of Piraus or in Tarent. The comparison with the man on top machine clearly indicates the dimensions of this flying boat. Here too, the emblem can be seen, and to the right of it coding, and left at the nose the double circle with BV, the emblem of the manufacturer Blohm & Voss. Only twelve BV 222s, V1 to V12 were built.

The Dornier Do 26, of which only six were built, was definitely the most elegant flying boat. These two photos show Do 26 V1 baptized "Sea Eagle" during Lufthansa Service, and as Luftwaffe code P5+AH, it formerly serviced Lufthansa's South-Atlantic lines. It is seen here in Rombakkenfjord at end of May 1940 during the Norwegian campaign. It belonged to the special transocean Transozean KGr.z.b.V. 108. Staffelkapitän Major von Buddenbrock is seen between the two rear engines. Pilot was Ernst Wilhelm Modrow, later awarded the Knight's Cross for his successes as a nightfighter flying the He 219. On May 28, 1940 at 1750 hours British aircraft destroyed the Do 26s V1 and V4.

A He 59 of German SAR taxies into the Potenitzer Wick of Travemunde in 1940. The aircraft stili displays the civilian marking D-AROO, and has a big red cross instead of the Balkenkreuz. The drop-shaped attachment under the nose seems to be a searchlight.

Above and opposite below: A Do 24T is lifted off the slipcart to be launched. The code could be K6+??, which means this aircraft could belong to Ku.Fl.Gr.406. With the Do 24T the Luftwaffe was provided with a sea-going reconnaissance, transport and SAR flying boat, that was equipped with three revolving turrets.

Heinkel's He 42 was developed in 1931 as a floatplane for pilot training. Due to its sturdy construction it proved highly qualified for this task. This He 42, code SD+??, shown here resting on a slipcart at Keil-Holtenau, does not belong to a school but was part of Ld.Kdo.65 Within the Luftwaffe, these units were so-called "maids of all work", and their main task was target-tug for the navy. This photo dates to around 1938.

Pictured also at Kiel-Hontenau around 1938 was this He 60, coded NO+FX. Despite the fact that it is not marked with the LD.-triangle like the He 42, it also belongs to Ld.Kdo.65. Some sort of emblem is visible, reminiscent of a coastal patrol unit. Note the "4" on the rudder.

For its Atlantic flights from Bathurst/Africa to Natal/Brazil, Lufthansa used the modern Do 18, successor of the Dornier Wal. These machines were all named after meterological winds, the one pictured here parking at Bathurst some time in 1938, code D-ARUN, was baptized "Zephyr".

Here the D-ARUN on the carapult of the Air traffic contol vessel "Ostmark", on constant position in the South Atlantic halfway between Africa and Brazil. Lufthansa flying boats en route to or from Brazil made a stop-over at the vessel. The aircraft was taken aboard, refuelled and then catapulted.

Chapter 10

Foreign Aircraft in Luftwaffe Service

This chapter only deals with aircraft not developed by the German aviation industry. A majority of these aircraft were captured on a variety of war fronts. Also noted are enemy aircraft that crash landed in German held territory, as well as the aircraft of Austria and Czechoslovakia after their annexation.

Students of the fighter training group of JG 107 in Hungary had lots of fun with this captured Czechoslovakian Avia Fl 3, coded BU+LI. In the background a Bf 109G of the fighter school. This photo was taken in September 1944.

A Czechoslovakian Avia B 122 of A/B 4 at Neudorf/Oppeln just before take-off in Summer 1941. BO+IK displays the school emblem with the funnel on the fuselage between the wings. One student reported that this aircraft was used mainly for high altitude flights after he managed an emergency landing after engine trouble at 3000 meters.

Numerous aircraft were captured during the occupation of Czechoslovakia and turned-over to the Luftwaffe. One was this Avia B 122 with a Walter-Castor engine. This photo was taken in spring 1939 at an unknown airfield.

Flight instructor Henri Asmus with one of his trainer aircraft, Avia B534, code TC+??, of A/B 114 Wien-Zwolfaxing. At the schools this type was flown as a so-called K-type, to give the students a taste of fighter training.

This Czech Avia Bk 534 was flown in the summer of 1940 at the flight instructor school at Brandenburg-Briest. When all of Czecho-slovakia was occupied, a great number of this type were captured and assigned to schools and fighter squadrons, such as JG 71. Shown here is CR+AV "White 3."

A Benes-Mraz Be 51 "Beta Minor" of A/B 71 Prossnitz during take-off in winter 1942/43. Note that GA+ABs wheelspats were removed and the engine cowling changed. Other publications show this same aircraft with the black stripes extended to the spinner.

Another Benes-MRAZ Be 51 was used at A/B 119 Kassel-Rothwesten. ?K+IH clearly shows the seat arrangement of this two-seat trainer. Note the raised rear canopy glazing.

In the summer of 1941 the A/B 4 Neudorf/Oppeln also had a Benes-Mraz 51 in its inventory. The so-called "pleasure-bird" was used for occasional shopping trips. The inscription Beta Minor is immediately above the emblem.

A Bloch MB 152 at the French airfield at Cognac, 1940. Oblt. Baron von Hotley, Staffelkapitän of EJG 26 made some test flights with this aircraft.

After the French surrender a few Bloch 200s came to the German pilot schools despite the fact that this type did not make a good impression. At the beginning of the war the French air force was already hopelessly outdated.

A very rare aircraft in the German SAR squadrons was this French flying boat Breguet 521 Bizerte. This photo was taken in the summer of 1943 in the harbor of Marseille-Marignac. Note the lack of the white outline on the swastika and Balkenkreuz.

Interested soldiers view the famous 303rd Bomb Group Boeing B-17F "Flying Fortress", serial number 124584, that was forced to land at Leeuwarden, Holland. The German code DL+SC reveals that this aircraft either belonged to a Luftwaffe test unit or to the "Circus Rosarius."

This French Caudron C 445 "Goeland" was in the inventory of many pilot and radio operator schools. Developed as a commuter aircraft, it was now used together with Fw 58s for B-2 training, and as a flying classroom for radio operators. RC+YC was assigned to A/B Kassel-Rothwesten in 1943/44.

We do not know what happened to this C 445 of A/B 62 Bad Voslau, but it looks like an emergency landing due to engine trouble. The engine probably failed, and after the pilot landed the aircraft, the engine broke off. This happened frequently, as the Renault engines left this aircraft considerably underpowered.

Another C 445 was used in North Africa with I./St.G.1 as a courier aircraft. Painted on the nose of ??+YO is the "Diving Raven" group emblem. The dapple-pattern camouflage was used only with aircraft operating in the Mediterranean area.

Also used by the Luftwaffe was this Consolidated B-24H "Liberator", serial No. 252106, named "Sunshine" in the fall of 1944 at the Luftwaffe Radar Research Center at Werneuchen. According to Inspector Oskar Lamberts' flight log, the aircraft was flown by E-Stelle Werneuchen between August 2 and December 30, 1944. During this period Lamberts made thirty-five test flights in this B-24.

This picture clearly demonstrates the giant dimensions of the Liberator's main undercarriage. Members of E-Stelle Werneuchen inspect the rear section of the fuselage, left to right Mr. Heilmann, Dr. Goos and Inspector Lamberts. From this B-24 the first serviceable "Meddo" air-to-ground radar set fell into the hands of the E-Stelle, who were then occupied with the development of an improved version of the German radar-set H2S-"Rotteram." When they inspected the Meddo set it was found that it was technically superior to their own work.

This photo shows the pin-up-girl as "nose-art." Inspecting are (left to right) Mr. Heilmann, Dr. Goos, Inspector Lamberts. This photo was also taken in the fall of 1944 at Wernechen. Beneath the cockpit are fifteen bomb mission silhouettes painted on the fuselage. On its sixteenth mission the aircraft fell undamaged into German hands. When the aircraft was captured, and its whereabouts after December 1944 is unknown.

This Curtiss H 75, coded DS+NU was used for fighter training at the fighter school 4 Furth in Spring 1941. Some aircraft of this type belonged to the French air force and were captured during the French campaign.

Student pilot Uffz. Gennerich suffered only light injuries while his aircraft was damaged beyond repair. After dogfight training with his Dewoitine D 520 and turning-into land he touched ground and crashed. He and his aircraft, code ?V+M? belonged to JG 101 at Pau, France in Spring 1943.

JG 101 at Pau, France had many Dewoitine D 520 for fighter training. During the French campaign this aircraft was the most modern fighter in the French air force, almost reaching Bf 109 standards. However, the limited number in the French units had no chance against German air superiority. These two photo show two different D 520s in the fall of 1943.

The biplane Fiat CR 32, shown here of JG 106 at Lachen-Speyerdorf, was a very maneuverable fighter among the various types of training aircraft. This type was very successful during the Spanish Civil War. Note the spoked wheels, the original spats had been removed.

During the Battle of Britain some fighter missions were flown by Italian airforce units equipped with the biplane Fiat CR 42 bis. Shown here in Belgium, this photo shows this type with German markings and insignia and probably belonging to a fighter school.

When Holland was occupied, a number of Fokker G-1s fell into German hands. Classified as expendable, they were allocated to German flying schools. In this configuration it is similar to the Fw 189, and was designated as a heavy destroyer.

This photo shows a Fokker D-XXI, a former Dutch fighter, in German marking and interesting camouflage. With its fixed undercarriage it was not a very promising type.

In the spring of 1940, the flying students of FAR 31 at Pilsen made also trained on the Letov S 328. NX+?? still has bomb racks underwing, which indicate the former tasks of this aircraft.

At the A/B 32 Pardibitz pilot Peter Ludcke, the "Oxkiller", was in action. In August 1941 Ludcke, while approaching the airstrip of Chrudin with his Letov S 328, touched a crossing oxcart. Result: two dead oxen, and one aircraft damaged beyond repair, as can be seen here. Note the laminated propeller blades, the school emblem and the manufacturer's markings S 328.221.

During the period August 1941 until May 1942 a Hawker Hurricane coded ?F+SC, was assigned to I./JFS 2 Zerbst/Anhalt for training purposes. This enabled fighter students to perform comparative flights with this British fighter. The Hurricane by this time was obsolete, and most RAF units reequipped with the Spitfire.

In Fall 1940 at the Channel Front, II./JG 51 also had a Hurricane for comparative flights. It was not used for combat missions. This photo shows the aircraft taxiing to its take-off point.

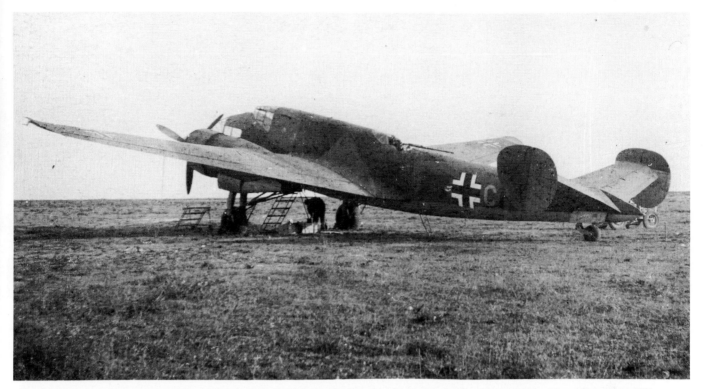

Many light bombers of the type Loire et Olivier LeO 451 fell into German hands during the French campaign. The yellow letter "C" and the adjoining black letter indicate the marking of an operational unit. The LeO 451 was one of the few captured aircraft integrated into Luftwaffe. With German national insignia, Balkenkreuz, unit marking, German defense weapons and Luftwaffe crew, they flew combat missions. The photo was probably taken towards the end of 1943 at Montepellier, France.

Pilot Otto Deelig of trials unit Ob.d.I. posing with a captured Lockheed P-38 "Lightning" in 1942 at an airstrip near Rome, Italy. Note the painted-over U.S. markings on the tailbooms.

After the French campaign a great number of North American NAA 64s fell into the hands of the Luftwaffe who allocated them to its various flying schools. This photo was taken of May 27, 1941 and shows DS+QG of fighter preschool 2 Lachenspeyerdorf still displaying its original finish.

This NAA 57, coded KR+??, and allocated to Stuka preschool Bad Aibling in 1940/41, has a new finish.

Shown here is the old Morane Saulnier MS 230, code DS+RV , spending its last days in December 1940 at FFS A/B 24 Olmutz. The underside of the aircraft is painted all over yellow. Not that the swastika has open ends.

Morane Saulnier MS 406, a standard French fighter aircraft, shown here at 1./JFS 5 Liehescourt, France in the summer of 1941, displaying code DS+?? It also has a yellow underside, for identification.

Also frequently seen at pilot schools was the Czechoslovakian Praga E 39, shown here at the A/B 23 Juterbog/Damm in 1940. Note that its lower wing has a wider span that the upper!

This hard landing occurred in 1941 at the FFS A/B 32 Pardubitz. Since their is only light damage, the VB+SI will soon be serviceable again. The school emblem is visible near the broken strut.

This photo taken in Winter 1940/41 at FFS A/B Wels and shows a line of Czechoslovakian Praga E 39 training aircraft.

Another Czechoslovakian aircraft type in the service of German flying schools was this Praga E 241, shown here ready for take-off at the airstrip Perrau of A/B 24 Olmutz. This photo shows the biplane coded NO+ZD with its extensive bracing.

Photographed in July-August 1944 at Reinsehlen is this U.S. Republic P-47 "Thunderbolt," which now belongs to the "Circus Rosarius" and is coded T9+PK. The Circus Rosarius was the official nick-name of a special trials unit of the High Command of the Luftwaffe, as the P-47 code T9 reveals.

Many "funny birds" were among the Luftwaffe units. In Spring 1944 at the A/B 14 Klagenfurt this Italian Meridionali Romeo Ro 41 was flown, an aircraft that had already flown in the Spanish Civil War in small numbers. In front of the aircraft is flying student Karl-Heinz Kabus (left).

This photo also shows another aircraft of the Circus Rosarius, a Spitfire, probably a Mk.XI. In this photo the "Circus" visited II./JG 26 at Reinsehlen/Luneberg Heath in July-August 1944.

This Italian Savoia Marchetti SM 81 was integrated into German transport units. The one depicted here was coded 8Q+CW and displayed the tactical marking Z 5 W, which designated it as belonging to the Savoia squadron, 5. Staffel of III./KG.z.b.V. In May 1943 it was attached to Tr.Fl.St.4.

After the capitulation of Italy, the Luftwaffe greatly appreciated the integration of the large SM 82 into its transport units. The aircraft in this photo belonged to 2. Staffel of an unknown II. Transportgruppe. Two letters in its Staffel marking are applied aft of the Balkenkreuz and on the rudder.

Another SM 82, DL+FD. As with the one above it could belong to Savoia Staffel of KG.z.b.V.1, later TG 1 or Tr.Fl.St.4.

This photo shows a Tupolev SB-2, coded LP+FB. The unit is unidentified. This type of captured aircraft was used in Luftwaffe service mainly as a training target or target tug.

This snow-covered Yakovlev UT-1 was parked in a corner of the airfield of Pleskau during the Demjansk supply missions at the beginning of 1942.

284

This aircraft understandably attracts the attention of numerous members of the Luftwaffe. On November 7, 1941 at 1847 hours this Vickers Wellington Mk IV, GR-Z Serial No. 12772, of Number 301 Polish Squadron took off from Hemswell airfield in England on a bombing mission to Mannheim. On the way back the aircraft crossed the German occupied airfield at Eeekloo, Belgium. The German airfield crew assumed that one of their own aircraft was returning from a night mission, and subsequently turned on the airfield lights. The Polish crew mistook it as their home base and landed, where they were soon taken prisoner. The fate of the aircraft is unknown. However, the code GR+?? and the swastika could indicate that it was already allocated to a Luftwaffe trials unit. Two emblems are visible on the nose: the red-and-white emblem was the emblem of the Polish units in the RAF, the lion could be the city emblem of Torun or Thorn.

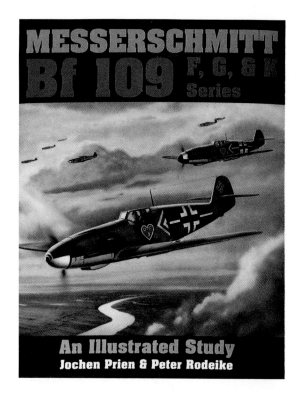

MESSERSCHMITT Me 262 • Development /Testing/Production Willy Radinger & Walter Schick. Detailed account of the technical developments of the fighter, fighter/bomber, reconnaissance, and night fighter versions of this classic design.
Size: 8 1/2" x 11"   112 pages hard cover
over 150 b/w, and 30 color photographs, documents
ISBN: 0-88740-516-9 $24.95

MESSERSCHMITT Bf 109 F/G/K Series • An Illustrated Study Jochen Prien & Peter Rodeike. The main thrust of this classic study is on the salient differences in the late production 109s. Detailed captions also present the color schemes, pilots, and locations of the photos shown.
Size: 8 1/2" x 11"   208 pages, over 490 b/w and color photographs, over 50 line drawings
ISBN: 0-88740-424-3   hard cover $35.00

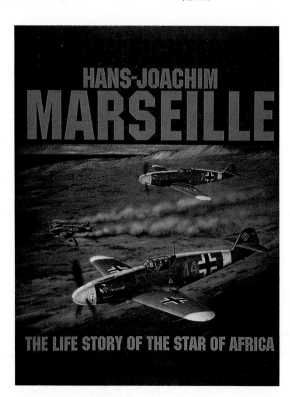

GERMAN FIGHTER ACE HANS-JOACHIM MARSEILLE • The Life Story of the "Star of Africa" Franz Kurowski. Biography of one of the top fighter aces of World War II. Also chronicled is the combat life of JG 27, Marseille's unit.
Size: 8 1/2" x 11"   256 pages over 200 b/w photos
ISBN: 0-88740-517-7 hard cover $39.95

GERMAN AIRCRAFT LANDING GEAR A Detailed Study of German World War II Combat Aircraft Günther Sengfelder. Detailed book explores the landing gear systems of World War II German combat aircraft.
Size: 8 1/2" x 11"
Hard cover, 246 pages, over 250 photographs, over 250 line schemes and cut-away drawings
ISBN: 0-88740-470-7 $35.00

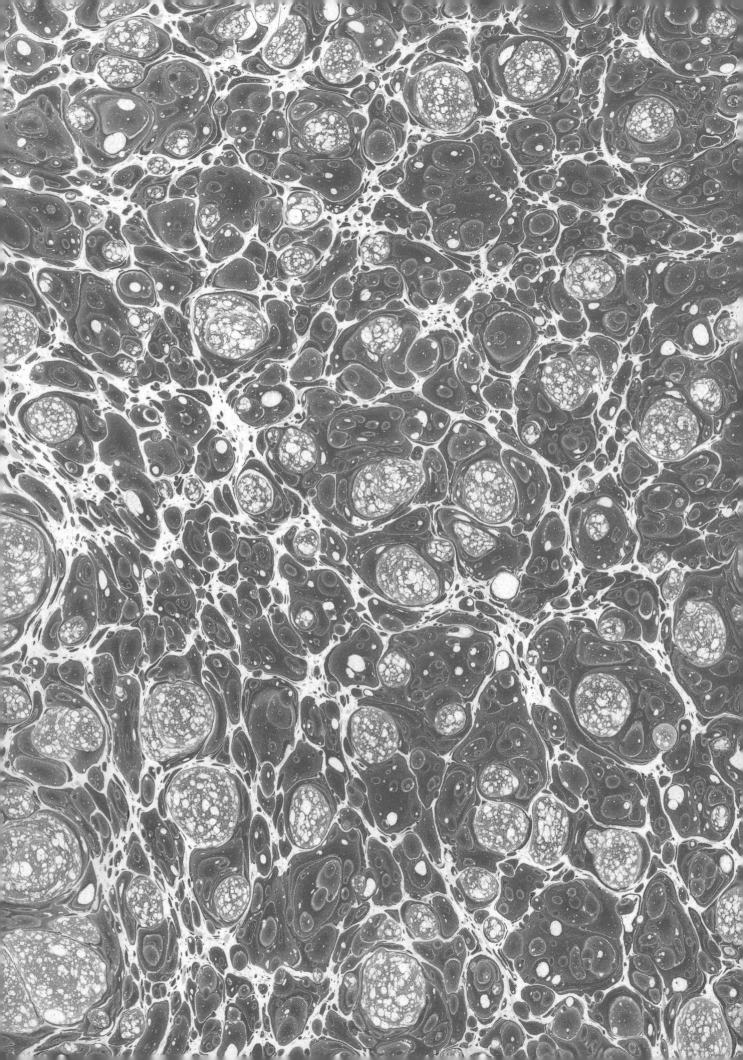